MANHATTAN PREP

Word Problems

GRE® Strategy Guide

The Word Problems guide educates students in the art of translating challenging word problems into organized data, as well as providing structured frameworks for attacking each question type.

guide **5**

Word Problems GRE Strategy Guide, Fourth Edition

10-digit International Standard Book Number: 1-937707-90-3
13-digit International Standard Book Number: 978-1-937707-90-3
eISBN: 978-1-937707-18-7

Layout Design: Dan McNaney and Cathy Huang
Cover Design: Dan McNaney and Frank Callaghan
Cover Photography: Sam Edla

SUSTAINABLE FORESTRY INITIATIVE Certified Sourcing
www.sfiprogram.org
SFI-00756

GRE STRATEGY GUIDES

STRATEGY GUIDE SUPPLEMENTS

MANHATTAN
PREP

June 3rd, 2014

Dear Student,

Thank you for picking up a copy of GRE *Word Problems*. I hope this book provides just the guidance you need to get the most out of your GRE studies.

As with most accomplishments, there were many people involved in the creation of the book you are holding. First and foremost is Zeke Vanderhoek, the founder of Manhattan Prep. Zeke was a lone tutor in New York when he started the company in 2000. Now, 14 years later, the company has instructors and offices nationwide and contributes to the studies and successes of thousands of GRE, GMAT, LSAT, and SAT students each year.

Our Manhattan Prep Strategy Guides are based on the continuing experiences of our instructors and students. We are particularly indebted to our instructors Stacey Koprince, Dave Mahler, Liz Ghini Moliski, Emily Meredith Sledge, and Tommy Wallach for their hard work on this edition. Dan McNaney and Cathy Huang provided their design expertise to make the books as user-friendly as possible, and Liz Krisher made sure all the moving pieces came together at just the right time. Beyond providing additions and edits for this book, Chris Ryan and Noah Teitelbaum continue to be the driving force behind all of our curriculum efforts. Their leadership is invaluable. Finally, thank you to all of the Manhattan Prep students who have provided input and feedback over the years. This book wouldn't be half of what it is without your voice.

At Manhattan Prep, we continually aspire to provide the best instructors and resources possible. We hope that you will find our commitment manifest in this book. If you have any questions or comments, please email me at dgonzalez@manhattanprep.com. I'll look forward to reading your comments, and I'll be sure to pass them along to our curriculum team.

Thanks again, and best of luck preparing for the GRE!

Sincerely,

Dan Gonzalez
President
Manhattan Prep

HOW TO ACCESS YOUR ONLINE RESOURCES

If you…

⊙ **are a registered Manhattan Prep GRE® student**

and have received this book as part of your course materials, you have AUTOMATIC access to ALL of our online resources. This includes all practice exams, question banks, and online updates to this book. To access these resources, follow the instructions in the Welcome Guide provided to you at the start of your program. Do NOT follow the instructions below.

⊙ **purchased this book from the Manhattan Prep online store or at one of our centers**

1. Go to: www.manhattanprep.com/gre/studentcenter.

2. Log in using the username and password used when your account was set up.

⊙ **purchased this book at a retail location**

1. Create an account with Manhattan Prep at the website: www.manhattanprep.com/gre/createaccount.

2. Go to: www.manhattanprep.com/gre/access.

3. Follow the instructions on the screen.

Your online access begins on the day that you register your book at the above URL.

You only need to register your product ONCE at the above URL. To use your online resources any time AFTER you have completed the registration process, log in to the following URL: www.manhattanprep.com/gre/studentcenter.

Please note that online access is nontransferable. This means that only NEW and UNREGISTERED copies of the book will grant you online access. Previously used books will NOT provide any online resources.

⊙ **purchased an eBook version of this book**

1. Create an account with Manhattan Prep at the website: www.manhattanprep.com/gre/createaccount.

2. Email a copy of your purchase receipt to gre@manhattanprep.com to activate your resources. Please be sure to use the same email address to create an account that you used to purchase the eBook.

For any technical issues, email techsupport@manhattanprep.com or call 800-576-4628.

TABLE *of* CONTENTS

guide **5**

Chapter 1 *of* Word Problems

Introduction

In This Chapter...

The Revised GRE

Question Formats in Detail

Chapter 1

Introduction

We know that you're looking to succeed on the GRE so that you can go to graduate school and do the things you want to do in life.

We also know that you may not have done math since high school, and that you may never have learned words like "adumbrate" or "sangfroid." We know that it's going to take hard work on your part to get a top GRE score, and that's why we've put together the only set of books that will take you from the basics all the way up to the material you need to master for a near-perfect score, or whatever your goal score may be. You've taken the first step. Now it's time to get to work!

How to Use These Materials

Manhattan Prep's GRE materials are comprehensive. But keep in mind that, depending on your score goal, it may not be necessary to get absolutely everything. Grad schools only see your overall Quantitative, Verbal, and Writing scores—they don't see exactly which strengths and weaknesses went into creating those scores.

You may be enrolled in one of our courses, in which case you already have a syllabus telling you in what order you should approach the books. But if you bought this book online or at a bookstore, feel free to approach the books—and even the chapters within the books—in whatever order works best for you. For the most part, the books, and the chapters within them, are independent; you don't have to master one section before moving on to the next. So if you're having a hard time with something in particular, you can make a note to come back to it later and move on to another section. Similarly, it may not be necessary to solve every single practice problem for every section. As you go through the material, continually assess whether you understand and can apply the principles in each individual section and chapter. The best way to do this is to solve the Check Your Skills and Problem Sets throughout. If you're confident you have a concept or method down, feel free to move on. If you struggle with something, make note of it for further review. Stay active in your learning and stay oriented toward the test—it's easy to read something and think you understand it, only to have trouble applying it in the 1–2 minutes you have to solve a problem.

1

Study Skills

As you're studying for the GRE, try to integrate your learning into your everyday life. For example, vocabulary is a big part of the GRE, as well as something you just can't "cram" for—you're going to want to do at least a little bit of vocab every day. So try to learn and internalize a little bit at a time, switching up topics often to help keep things interesting.

Keep in mind that, while many of your study materials are on paper (including Education Testing Service's [ETS's] most recent source of official GRE questions, *The Official Guide to the GRE revised General Test, Second Edition*), your exam will be administered on a computer. Because this is a computer-based test, you will *not* be able to underline portions of reading passages, write on diagrams of geometry figures, or otherwise physically mark up problems. So get used to this now. Solve the problems in these books on scratch paper. (Each of our books talks specifically about what to write down for different problem types.)

Again, as you study, stay focused on the test-day experience. As you progress, work on timed drills and sets of questions. Eventually, you should be taking full practice tests (available at www.manhattanprep.com/gre) under actual timed conditions.

The Revised GRE

As of August 1, 2011, the Quantitative and Verbal sections of the GRE underwent a number of changes. The actual body of knowledge being tested is more or less the same as it ever was, but the *way* that knowledge is tested changed. Here's a brief summary of the changes, followed by a more comprehensive assessment of the new exam.

The current test is a little longer than the old test, lengthened from about 3.5 hours to about 4 hours. When you sign up for the exam at www.ets.org/gre, you will be told to plan to be at the center for 5 hours, since there will be some paperwork to complete when you arrive, and occasionally test-takers are made to wait a bit before being allowed to begin.

Taking a four-hour exam can be quite exhausting, so it's important to practice not only out of these books, but also on full-length computer-based practice exams, such as the exam available with your online resources.

There are now two scored Quantitative sections and two scored Verbal sections. A new score scale of 130–170 is used in place of the old 200–800 scale. More on this later.

The Verbal section of the GRE changed dramatically. The Antonyms and Analogies disappeared. The Text Completion and Reading Comprehension remain, expanded and remixed in a few new ways. Vocabulary is still important, but is tested only in the context of complete sentences.

MANHATTAN
PREP

The Quant section of the new GRE still contains the same multiple-choice problems, Quantitative Comparisons, and Data Interpretations (which are really a subset of multiple-choice problems). The revised test also contains two new problem formats, which we will introduce in this section.

On both Verbal and Quant, some of the new question types have more than one correct answer, or otherwise break out of the mold of traditional multiple-choice exams. You might say that computer-based exams are finally taking advantage of the features of computers.

One way that this is true is that the new exam includes a small, on-screen, four-function calculator with a square root button. Many test-takers will rejoice at the advent of this calculator. It is true that the GRE calculator will reduce emphasis on computation—but look out for problems, such as percents questions with tricky wording, that are likely to foil those who rely on the calculator too much. *In short, the calculator may make your life a bit easier from time to time, but it's not a game changer.* There are **zero** questions that can be solved *entirely* with a calculator. You will still need to know the principles contained in the six Quant books (of the eight-book Manhattan Prep GRE series).

Finally, don't worry about whether the new GRE is harder or easier than the old GRE. You are being judged against other test-takers, all of whom are in the same boat. So if the new formats are harder, they are harder for other test-takers as well.

Additionally, graduate schools to which you will be applying have been provided with conversion charts so that applicants with old and new GRE scores can be compared fairly (GRE scores are valid for five years).

Exam Structure

The revised test has six sections. You will get a 10-minute break between the third and fourth sections and a 1-minute break between the others. The Analytical Writing section is always first. The other five sections can be seen in any order and will include:

- Two Verbal Reasoning sections (20 questions each in 30 minutes per section)
- Two Quantitative Reasoning sections (20 questions each in 35 minutes per section)
- Either an unscored section or a research section

An unscored section will look just like a third Verbal or Quantitative Reasoning section, and you will not be told which of them doesn't count. If you get a research section, it will be identified as such, and will be the last section you get.

Section #	Section Type	# Questions	Time	Scored?
1	Analytical Writing	2 essays	30 minutes each	Yes
2	Verbal #1	Approx. 20	30 minutes	Yes
3	Quantitative #1 *(order can vary)*	Approx. 20	35 minutes	Yes
10-Minute Break				
4	Verbal #2	Approx. 20	30 minutes	Yes
5	Quantitative #2 *(order can vary)*	Approx. 20	35 minutes	Yes
?	Unscored Section *(Verbal or Quant, order can vary)*	Approx. 20	30 or 35 minutes	No
Last	Research Section	Varies	Varies	No

All the question formats will be looked at in detail later in the chapter.

Using the Calculator

The addition of a small, four-function calculator with a square root button means that re-memorizing times tables or square roots is less important than it used to be. However, the calculator is not a cure-all; in many problems, the difficulty is in figuring out what numbers to put into the calculator in the first place. In some cases, using a calculator will actually be less helpful than doing the problem some other way. Take a look at an example:

> If x is the remainder when (11)(7) is divided by 4 and y is the remainder when (14)
> (6) is divided by 13, what is the value of $x + y$?

Solution: This problem is designed so that the calculator won't tell the whole story. Certainly, the calculator will tell you that $11 \times 7 = 77$. When you divide 77 by 4, however, the calculator yields an answer of 19.25. The remainder is not 0.25 (a remainder is always a whole number).

You might just go back to your pencil and paper, and find the largest multiple of 4 that is less than 77. Since 4 does go into 76, you can conclude that 4 would leave a remainder of 1 when dividing into 77.

1

(Notice that you don't even need to know how many times 4 goes into 76, just that it goes in. One way to mentally "jump" to 76 is to say, 4 goes into 40, so it goes into 80…that's a bit too big, so take away 4 to get 76.)

However, it is also possible to use the calculator to find a remainder. Divide 77 by 4 to get 19.25. Thus, 4 goes into 77 nineteen times, with a remainder left over. Now use your calculator to multiply 19 (JUST 19, not 19.25) by 4. You will get 76. The remainder is $77 - 76$, which is 1. Therefore, $x = 1$. You could also multiply the leftover 0.25 times 4 (the divisor) to find the remainder of 1.

Use the same technique to find y. Multiply 14 by 6 to get 84. Divide 84 by 13 to get 6.46. Ignore everything after the decimal, and just multiply 6 by 13 to get 78. The remainder is therefore $84 - 78$, which is 6. Therefore, $y = 6$.

Since you are looking for $x + y$, and $1 + 6 = 7$, the answer is 7.

You can see that blind faith in the calculator can be dangerous. Use it responsibly! And this leads us to…

Practice Using the Calculator!

On the revised GRE, the on-screen calculator will slow you down or lead to incorrect answers if you're not careful! If you plan to use it on test day (which you should), you'll want to practice first.

We have created an online practice calculator for you to use. To access this calculator, go to www.manhattanprep.com/gre and sign in to the student center using the instructions on the "How to Access Your Online Resources" page found at the front of this book.

Throughout our math books, you will see the symbol. This symbol means "Use the calculator here!" As much as possible, have the online practice calculator up and running during your review of our math books. You'll have the chance to use the on-screen calculator when you take our practice exams as well.

Navigating the Questions in a Section

Another change for test-takers on the revised GRE is the ability to move freely around the questions in a section—you can go forward and backward one-by-one and can even jump directly to any question from the "review list." The review list provides a snapshot of which questions you have answered, which ones you have tagged for "mark and review," and which are incomplete, either because you didn't indicate enough answers or because you indicated too many (that is, if a number of choices is specified by the question). You should double-check the review list for completion if you finish the section early. Using the review list feature will take some practice as well, which is why we've built it into our online practice exams.

1

The majority of test-takers will be pressed for time. Thus, for some, it won't be feasible to go back to multiple problems at the end of the section. Generally, if you can't get a question the first time, you won't be able to get it the second time around either. With this in mind, here's the order in which we recommend using the new review list feature.

1. Do the questions in the order in which they appear.

2. When you encounter a difficult question, do your best to eliminate answer choices you know are wrong.

3. If you're not sure of an answer, take an educated guess from the choices remaining. Do NOT skip it and hope to return to it later.

4. Using the "mark" button at the top of the screen, mark up to three questions per section that you think you might be able to solve with more time. Mark a question only after you have taken an educated guess.

5. Always click on the review list at the end of a section, to quickly make sure you have neither skipped nor incompletely answered any questions.

6. If you have time, identify any questions that you marked for review and return to them. If you do not have any time remaining, you will have already taken good guesses at the tough ones.

What you want to avoid is surfing—clicking forward and backward through the questions searching for the easy ones. This will eat up valuable time. Of course, you'll want to move through the tough ones quickly if you can't get them, but try to avoid skipping around.

Again, all of this will take practice. Use our practice exams to fine-tune your approach.

Scoring

You need to know two things about the scoring of the revised GRE Verbal Reasoning and Quantitative Reasoning sections: (1) how individual questions influence the score, and (2) the score scale itself.

For both the Verbal Reasoning and Quantitative Reasoning sections, you will receive a scaled score, based on both how many questions you answered correctly and the difficulties of the specific questions you actually saw.

The old GRE was question-adaptive, meaning that your answer to each question (right or wrong) determined, at least somewhat, the questions that followed (harder or easier). Because you had to commit to an answer to let the algorithm do its thing, you weren't allowed to skip questions or to go back to change answers. On the revised GRE, the adapting occurs from section to section rather than from question to question (e.g., if you do well on the first Verbal section, you will get a harder second Verbal section). The only change test-takers will notice is one that most will welcome: you can now move freely about the questions in a section, coming back to tough questions later, changing answers after "Aha!" moments, and generally managing your time more flexibly.

1

The scores for the revised GRE Quantitative Reasoning and Verbal Reasoning are reported on a 130–170 scale in 1-point increments, whereas the old score reporting was on a 200–800 scale in 10-point increments. You will receive one 130–170 score for Verbal and a separate 130–170 score for Quant. If you are already putting your GRE math skills to work, you may notice that there are now 41 scores possible (170 − 130, then add 1 before you're done), whereas before there were 61 scores possible ([800 − 200]/10, then add 1 before you're done). In other words, a 10-point difference on the old score scale actually indicated a smaller performance differential than a 1-point difference on the new scale. However, the GRE folks argue that perception is reality: the difference between 520 and 530 on the old scale could simply seem greater than the difference between 151 and 152 on the new scale. If that's true, then this change will benefit test-takers, who won't be unfairly compared by schools for minor differences in performance. If not true, then the change is moot.

Question Formats in Detail

Essay Questions

The Analytical Writing section consists of two separately timed 30-minute tasks: Analyze an Issue and Analyze an Argument. As you can imagine, the 30-minute time limit implies that you aren't aiming to write an essay that would garner a Pulitzer Prize nomination, but rather to complete the tasks adequately and according to the directions. Each essay is scored separately, but your reported essay score is the average of the two, rounded up to the next half-point increment on a 0–6 scale.

Issue Task: This essay prompt will present a claim, generally one that is vague enough to be interpreted in various ways and discussed from numerous perspectives. Your job as a test-taker is to write a response discussing the extent to which you agree or disagree and support your position. Don't sit on the fence—pick a side!

For some examples of Issue Task prompts, visit the GRE website here:

> www.ets.org/gre/revised_general/prepare/analytical_writing/issue/pool

Argument Task: This essay prompt will be an argument comprised of both a claim (or claims) and evidence. Your job is to dispassionately discuss the argument's structural flaws and merits (well, mostly the flaws). Don't agree or disagree with the argument—simply evaluate its logic.

For some examples of Argument Task prompts, visit the GRE website here:

> www.ets.org/gre/revised_general/prepare/analytical_writing/argument/pool

Verbal: Reading Comprehension Questions

Standard five-choice multiple-choice Reading Comprehension questions continue to appear on the revised exam. You are likely familiar with how these work. Let's take a look at two *new* Reading Comprehension formats that will appear on the revised test.

Select One or More Answer Choices and Select-in-Passage

For the question type "Select One or More Answer Choices," you are given three statements about a passage and asked to "indicate all that apply." Either one, two, or all three can be correct (there is no "none of the above" option). There is no partial credit; you must indicate all of the correct choices and none of the incorrect choices.

Strategy Tip: On "Select One or More Answer Choices," don't let your brain be tricked into telling you, "Well, if two of them have been right so far, the other one must be wrong," or any other arbitrary idea about how many of the choices *should* be correct. Make sure to consider each choice independently! You cannot use "process of elimination" in the same way as you do on normal multiple-choice questions.

For the question type "Select-in-Passage," you are given an assignment such as "Select the sentence in the passage that explains why the experiment's results were discovered to be invalid." Clicking anywhere on the sentence in the passage will highlight it. (As with any GRE question, you will have to click "Confirm" to submit your answer, so don't worry about accidentally selecting the wrong sentence due to a slip of the mouse.)

Strategy Tip: On "Select-in-Passage," if the passage is short, consider numbering each sentence (i.e., writing 1 2 3 4 on your paper) and crossing off each choice as you determine that it isn't the answer. If the passage is long, you might write a number for each paragraph (I, II, III), and tick off each number as you determine that the correct sentence is not located in that paragraph.

Now give these new question types a try:

The sample questions below are based on this passage:

> Physicist Robert Oppenheimer, director of the fateful Manhattan Project, said, "It is a profound and necessary truth that the deep things in science are not found because they are useful; they are found because it was possible to find them." In a later address at MIT, Oppenheimer presented the thesis that scientists could be held only very nominally responsible for the consequences of their research and discovery. Oppenheimer asserted that ethics, philosophy, and politics have very little to do with the day-to-day work of the scientist, and that scientists could not rationally be expected to predict all the effects of their work. Yet, in a talk in 1945 to the Association of Los Alamos Scientists, Oppenheimer offered some reasons why the Manhattan Project scientists built the atomic bomb; the justifications included "fear that Nazi Germany would build it first" and "hope that it would shorten the war."

MANHATTAN
PREP

For question #1, consider each of the three choices separately and indicate all that apply.

1.   The passage implies that Robert Oppenheimer would most likely have agreed with which of the following views:

   A   Some scientists take military goals into account in their work
   B   Deep things in science are not useful
   C   The everyday work of a scientist is only minimally involved with ethics

2.   Select the sentence in which the writer implies that Oppenheimer has not been consistent in his view that scientists have little consideration for the effects of their work.

(Here, you would highlight the appropriate sentence with your mouse. Note that there are only four options.)

Solutions

1. **(A)** and **(C):** Oppenheimer says in the last sentence that one of the reasons the bomb was built was scientists' *hope that it would shorten the war.* Thus, Oppenheimer would likely agree with the view that *Some scientists take military goals into account in their work.* (B) is a trap answer using familiar language from the passage. Oppenheimer says that scientific discoveries' possible usefulness is not why scientists make discoveries; he does not say that the discoveries aren't useful. Oppenheimer specifically says that ethics has *very little to do with the day-to-day work of the scientist,* which is a good match for *only minimally involved with ethics.*

Strategy Tip: On "Select One or More Answer Choices," write A B C on your paper and mark each choice with a check, an *X*, or a symbol such as ~ if you're not sure. This should keep you from crossing out all three choices and having to go back (at least one of the choices must be correct). For example, say that on a *different* question you had marked

   A. *X*
   B. ~
   C. *X*

The answer choice you weren't sure about, (B), is likely to be correct, since there must be at least one correct answer.

---

2. The correct sentence is: **Yet, in a talk in 1945 to the Association of Los Alamos Scientists, Oppenheimer offered some reasons why the Manhattan Project scientists built the atomic bomb; the justifications included "fear that Nazi Germany would build it first" and "hope that it would shorten the war."** The word "yet" is a good clue that this sentence is about to express a view contrary to the views expressed in the rest of the passage.

1

Verbal: Text Completion Questions

Text Completions can consist of 1–5 sentences with 1–3 blanks. When Text Completions have two or three blanks, you will select words or short phrases for those blanks independently. There is no partial credit; you must make every selection correctly.

> Leaders are not always expected to (i) _____ the same rules as are those they lead; leaders are often looked up to for a surety and presumption that would be viewed as (ii) _____ in most others.

Blank (i)	Blank (ii)
decree	hubris
proscribe	avarice
conform to	anachronism

Select your two choices by actually clicking and highlighting the words you want.

Solution

In the first blank, you need a word similar to "follow." In the second blank, you need a word similar to "arrogance." The correct answers are *conform to* and *hubris*.

Strategy Tip: Do NOT look at the answer choices until you've decided for yourself, based on textual clues actually written in the sentence, what kind of word needs to go in each blank. Only then should you look at the choices and eliminate those that are not matches.

Now try an example with three blanks:

> For Kant, the fact of having a right and having the (i) _____ to enforce it via coercion cannot be separated, and he asserts that this marriage of rights and coercion is compatible with the freedom of everyone. This is not at all peculiar from the standpoint of modern political thought—what good is a right if its violation triggers no enforcement (be it punishment or (ii) _____)? The necessity of coercion is not at all in conflict with the freedom of everyone, because this coercion only comes into play when someone has (iii) _____ someone else.

Blank (i)	Blank (ii)	Blank (iii)
technique	amortization	questioned the hypothesis of
license	reward	violated the rights of
prohibition	restitution	granted civil liberties to

MANHATTAN
PREP

1

Solution

In the first sentence, use the clue "he asserts that this marriage of rights and coercion is compatible with the freedom of everyone" to help fill in the first blank. Kant believes that "coercion" is "married to" rights and is compatible with freedom for all. So you want something in the first blank like "right" or "power." Kant believes that rights are meaningless without enforcement. Only the choice *license* can work (while a *license* can be physical, like a driver's license, *license* can also mean "right").

The second blank is part of the phrase "punishment or _____," which you are told is the "enforcement" resulting from the violation of a right. So the blank should be something, other than punishment, that constitutes enforcement against someone who violates a right. (More simply, it should be something bad.) Only *restitution* works. Restitution is compensating the victim in some way (perhaps monetarily or by returning stolen goods).

In the final sentence, "coercion only comes into play when someone has _____ someone else." Throughout the text, "coercion" means enforcement against someone who has violated the rights of someone else. The meaning is the same here. The answer is *violated the rights of*.

The complete and correct answer is this combination:

Blank (i)	Blank (ii)	Blank (iii)
license	restitution	violated the rights of

In theory, there are 3 × 3 × 3, or 27 possible ways to answer a three-blank Text Completion—and only one of those 27 ways is correct. In theory, these are bad odds. In practice, you will often have certainty about some of the blanks, so your guessing odds are almost never this bad. Just follow the basic process: come up with your own filler for each blank, and match to the answer choices. If you're confused by this example, don't worry! Our *GRE Text Completion & Sentence Equivalence* guide covers all of this in detail.

Strategy Tip: Do not write your own story. The GRE cannot give you a blank without also giving you a clue, physically written down in the passage, telling you what kind of word or phrase must go in that blank. Find that clue. You should be able to give textual evidence for each answer choice you select.

Verbal: Sentence Equivalence Questions

For this question type, you are given one sentence with a single blank. There are six answer choices, and you are asked to pick two choices that fit the blank and are alike in meaning.

Of the Verbal question types, this one depends the most on vocabulary and also yields the most to strategy.

1

No partial credit is given on Sentence Equivalence; both correct answers must be selected and no incorrect answers may be selected. When you pick 2 of 6 choices, there are 15 possible combinations of choices, and only one is correct. However, this is not nearly as daunting as it sounds.

Think of it this way: if you have six choices, but the two correct ones must be similar in meaning, then you have, at most, three possible *pairs* of choices, maybe fewer, since not all choices are guaranteed to have a partner. If you can match up the pairs, you can seriously narrow down your options.

Here is a sample set of answer choices:

- [A] tractable
- [B] taciturn
- [C] arbitrary
- [D] tantamount
- [E] reticent
- [F] amenable

The question is deliberately omitted here in order to illustrate how much you can do with the choices alone, if you have studied vocabulary sufficiently.

Tractable and *amenable* are synonyms (tractable, amenable people will do whatever you want them to do). *Taciturn* and *reticent* are synonyms (both mean "not talkative").

Arbitrary (based on one's own will) and *tantamount* (equivalent) are not similar in meaning and therefore cannot be a pair. Therefore, the *only* possible correct answer pairs are (A) and (F), and (B) and (E). You have improved your chances from 1 in 15 to a 50/50 shot without even reading the question!

Of course, in approaching a Sentence Equivalence, you do want to analyze the sentence in the same way you would a Text Completion—read for a textual clue that tells you what type of word *must* go in the blank. Then look for a matching pair.

Strategy Tip: If you're sure that a word in the choices does *not* have a partner, cross it out! For instance, if (A) and (F) are partners and (B) and (E) are partners, and you're sure neither (C) nor (D) pair with any other answer, cross out (C) and (D) completely. They cannot be the answer together, nor can either one be part of the answer.

The sentence for the answer choice above could read as follows:

> Though the dinner guests were quite _____ , the hostess did her best to keep the conversation active and engaging.

Thus, **(B)** and **(E)** are the best choices.

MANHATTAN
PREP

Try another example:

While athletes usually expect to achieve their greatest feats in their teens or twenties, opera singers don't reach the _____ of their vocal powers until middle age.

       A   harmony
       B   zenith
       C   acme
       D   terminus
       E   nadir
       F   cessation

Solution

Those with strong vocabularies might go straight to the choices to make pairs. *Zenith* and *acme* are synonyms, meaning "high point, peak." *Terminus* and *cessation* are synonyms meaning "end." *Nadir* is a low point and *harmony* is present here as a trap answer reminding you of opera singers. Cross off (A) and (E), since they do not have partners. Then, go back to the sentence, knowing that your only options are a pair meaning "peak" and a pair meaning "end."

The correct answer choices are **(B)** and **(C)**.

Math: Quantitative Comparison

In addition to regular multiple-choice questions and Data Interpretation questions, Quantitative Comparisons have been on the exam for a long time.

Each question contains a "Quantity A" and a "Quantity B," and some also contain common information that applies to both quantities. The four answer choices are always worded exactly as shown in the following example:

$$x \geq 0$$

Quantity A	**Quantity B**
x	x^2

(A) Quantity A is greater.

(B) Quantity B is greater.

(C) The two quantities are equal.

(D) The relationship cannot be determined from the information given.

1

<u>Solution</u>

If $x = 0$, then the two quantities are equal. If $x = 2$, then Quantity (B) is greater. Thus, you don't have enough information.

The answer is **(D)**.

Next, take a look at the new math question formats.

Math: Select One or More Answer Choices

According to the *Official Guide to the GRE revised General Test*, the official directions for "Select One or More Answer Choices" read as follows:

> <u>Directions:</u> Select one or more answer choices according to the specific question directions.
>
> If the question does not specify how many answer choices to indicate, indicate all that apply.
>
> The correct answer may be just one of the choices or as many as all of the choices, depending on the question.
>
> No credit is given unless you indicate all of the correct choices and no others.
>
> If the question specifies how many answer choices to indicate, indicate exactly that number of choices.

Note that there is no partial credit. If three of six choices are correct, and you indicate two of the three, no credit is given. If you are told to indicate two choices and you indicate three, no credit is given. It will also be important to read the directions carefully.

Here's a sample question:

> If $ab = |a| \times |b|$ and $ab \neq 0$, which of the following must be true?
>
> Indicate <u>all</u> such statements.
>
> |A| $a = b$
> |B| $a > 0$ and $b > 0$
> |C| $ab > 0$

Note that only one, only two, or all three of the choices may be correct. (Also note the word "must" in the question stem!)

MANHATTAN
PREP

Solution

If $ab = |a| \times |b|$, then you know ab is positive, since the right side of the equation must be positive. If ab is positive, however, that doesn't necessarily mean that a and b are each positive; it simply means that they have the same sign.

Answer choice (A) is not correct because it is not true that a must equal b; for instance, a could be 2 and b could be 3.

Answer choice (B) is not correct because it is not true that a and b must each be positive; for instance, a could be -3 and b could be -4.

Now look at choice (C). Since $|a| \times |b|$ must be positive, ab must be positive as well; that is, since two sides of an equation are, by definition, equal to one another, if one side of the equation is positive, the other side must be positive as well. Thus, answer **(C)** is correct.

Strategy Tip: Make sure to fully process the statement in the question (simplify it or list the possible scenarios) before considering the answer choices. That is, don't just look at $ab = |a| \times |b|$—rather, it's your job to draw inferences about the statement before plowing ahead. This will save you time in the long run!

Note that "indicate all that apply" didn't really make the problem harder. This is just a typical Inference-based Quant problem (for more problems like this one, see our *GRE Number Properties* guide as well as our *GRE Quantitative Comparisons & Data Interpretation* guide).

After all, not every real-life problem has exactly five possible solutions; why should problems on the GRE?

Math: Numeric Entry

This question type requires the test-taker to key a numeric answer into a box on the screen. You are not able to work backwards from answer choices, and in many cases, it will be difficult to make a guess. However, the principles being tested are the same as on the rest of the exam.

Here is a sample question:

If $x \Delta y = 2xy - (x - y)$, what is the value of $3 \Delta 4$?

Solution

You are given a function involving two variables, x and y, and asked to substitute 3 for x and 4 for y:

$$x \Delta y = 2xy - (x - y)$$
$$3 \Delta 4 = 2(3)(4) - (3 - 4)$$
$$3 \Delta 4 = 24 - (-1)$$
$$3 \Delta 4 = 25$$

The answer is **25**.

Thus, you would type 25 into the box.

Okay. You've now got a good start on understanding the structure and question formats of the new GRE. Now it's time to begin fine-tuning your skills.

MANHATTAN
PREP

Chapter *of* 2

Word Problems

Algebraic Translations

In This Chapter...

Chapter 2
Algebraic Translations

Decoding the GRE Word Problem

Two thoughts are common to many frustrated students:

> "I don't know where to get started" and "I don't know what they want me to do."

You can attack these frustrations one at a time:

"I don't know where to get started."

A passive thinker takes in information, hopes that it will lead somewhere, waits for a connection to appear, and then… (hopefully)… voilà! In contrast, an active thinker *aggressively* seeks out relationships between the various elements of a problem and looks to write equations that can be solved. You have to be an active thinker on the GRE.

Here's a sample problem:

> A steel rod 50 meters long is cut into two pieces. If one piece is 14 meters longer than the other, what is the length, in meters, of the shorter piece?

The trick to word problems is to not try to do everything all at once. While it's great when the entire process is clear from the start, such clarity about your work is often not the case. That's why **you need to start by identifying unknowns and creating variables to represent the unknowns**. What quantities have you not been given specific values for? Take a moment to identify those quantities and write them down in the space provided below. Make up letters (variables) to stand for the quantities, and label these letters.

2

In this question, both the *length of the shorter piece* and the *length of the longer piece* are unknown, so begin by assigning each of those values a variable. You could go with the traditional algebraic variables x and y, but what if you forget which is which while you're busy answering the question? Instead, use letters that can help you remember which variable is assigned to which value:

S = length of the shorter piece

L = length of the longer piece

Just like that, you've gotten started on this problem. This may seem like a minor accomplishment in terms of the entire question, but it was an important one. Often, as soon as you start translating a word problem into *algebra*, the path forward becomes clearer. Now it's time to deal with the second frustration:

"I don't know what they want me to do."

Even now that you've identified and labeled your variables, you might still feel confused. That's fine. Virtually everyone ends up facing a number of problems that are above his or her ability level on the GRE. What distinguishes the higher-performing GRE test-takers in these moments is that they begin spelling out relationships before they know how the equations will prove useful. It's similar to untangling a ball of yarn: if you waited until you knew how the entire process would end, you might never get started. Of course, you hope to have a clear vision right from the start, but if you don't, *dive in and see what you find*—you'll likely make key realizations along the way. Ironically, often it's the roadblocks you encounter that point the way. So your next step is to **identify relationships and create equations**.

Go back to the problem, and look at *one piece of information at a time* and then *translate that information into equations*. Try it first on your own, then read on.

A steel rod 50 meters long is cut into two pieces.

The relationship expressed here is one of the two most common types of relationships found in Word Problems. The original length of the rod was 50 meters, and it was cut into 2 pieces. Therefore, the length of the shorter piece plus the length of the longer piece must equal 50 meters. This common relationship (one you should watch out for in other word problems) is **Parts Add to a Sum**. So a good way to express this relationship algebraically would be to write:

MANHATTAN
PREP

$S + L = 50$

Now that you've translated the first part of the problem, move on to the next part.

If one piece is 14 meters longer than the other …

The relationship expressed here is another common type found in word problems. The longer piece of metal is 14 meters longer than the shorter piece of metal. So if you were to add 14 meters to the shorter piece, it would be the same length as the longer piece. This relationship (be on the lookout for this one too) is **One Part Can Be Made Equal to the Other**. Either the question will say that two values are equivalent, or it will tell you exactly *how they differ.* This question told you how they were different, so your equation shows how you could make them equivalent. In this case, you would write:

$S + 14 = L$

By the way, when constructing equations in which you are making one part equal to the other, it can be very easy to express the relationship backwards. If you mistakenly wrote down S = L + 14, you're not alone. A good habit to get into if you find yourself making this kind of error is to verify your equation with **hypothetical numbers**. To check if the equation above is correct, start by imagining that the shorter piece of metal is 20 meters long. If the shorter piece were 20 meters long, then the longer piece would have to be 34 meters long. Now plug those numbers into your equation. Does 20 + 14 = 34? Yes, it does, so your equation is correct.

Next, move on to the final part of the question:

… what is the length, in meters, of the shorter piece?

This part of the question doesn't describe a relationship that you can use to create an equation, but it does tell you something quite useful: it tells you *what you're solving for!* Make sure that you note in some way what value you're actually looking for as you solve a problem—it can help you stay focused on the task at hand. In this problem, you're trying to find *S*. On your paper, you might even write:

$S = ?$

So now that you've **identified unknowns and created variables**, **identified relationships and created equations,** and **identified what the question is asking for**, it's time to put the pieces together and answer the question. Try it on your own first, and then when you have an answer, turn the page and you see the final steps.

2

First, you should recap, and then review the final steps and answer the question. After reading the question, you can create two equations:

$$S + L = 50$$
$$S + 14 = L$$

You have two variables and two equations, so you need to solve for S:

$$S + L = 50 \quad \rightarrow \quad L = 50 - S$$

$$S + 14 = (50 - S)$$
$$S + 14 = 50 - S$$
$$\,-14\,-14$$

$$S = 36 - S$$
$$+S\,+S$$
$$\frac{2S}{2} = \frac{36}{2}$$
$$S = 18$$

If you had trouble getting the correct value for S, then you should probably go back and refresh your algebra skills (see our *Algebra* guide). Knowing how to substitute and solve is absolutely essential if you want to do consistently well on Word Problems. If you're comfortable with everything you've done so far in order to answer the question, then you're ready for a tougher problem:

> Jack is 13 years older than Bao. In 8 years, he will be twice as old as Bao. How old is Jack now?

First try this problem on your own. Remember to follow the same steps you followed in the last question. After you're finished, review the explanation on the next page.

Ok, time to get started. The first thing you have to do is **identify unknowns** and **create variables**. In this problem, the two unknowns are the ages of Jack and Bao. You can represent them like this:

J = Jack's age *now*
B = Bao's age *now*

Before you move on to the next step, it's important to understand why you want to specify that the variables represent Jack and Bao's ages *now*. As you were solving this problem by yourself, you may have noticed that there was an added wrinkle to this question. You are presented with information that describes two distinct points in time—now and eight years from now. Some WPs on the GRE provide information about two distinct but related situations. When you are dealing with one of those problems, be careful about the reference point for your variables. In this case, you want to say that the variables represent Jack and Bao's ages *now* as opposed to eight years from now. This makes it easier to express their ages at other points in time.

Now that you've created variables, it's time to **identify relationships** and **create equations**. Go through the information presented in the question one piece at a time:

Jack is 13 years older than Bao.

Once again, check that you're putting this together the right way (not putting the +13 on the wrong side of the equation). Your equation should be:

$J = B + 13$, **NOT** $J + 13 = B$

Now, move on to the next piece of information:

In 8 years, he will be twice as old as Bao.

This piece is more challenging to translate than you might otherwise suspect. Remember, the variables represent their ages now, but this statement is talking about their ages 8 years from now. So you can't just write $J = 2B$. This relationship is dependent upon Jack and Bao's ages 8 years from now. You don't want to use new variables to represent these different ages, so adjust the values like this:

$(J + 8)$ = Jack's age 8 years from now
$(B + 8)$ = Bao's age 8 years from now

Now you can accurately create equations related to the earlier time *and* to the later time. Plus, if you keep those values in parentheses, then you can avoid potential PEMDAS errors! So your second equation should read:

$(J + 8) = 2(B + 8)$

Only one more piece of the question to go:

How old is Jack now?

This tells you that you're looking for the value of J. In other words, $J = ?$. All the pieces are in place and you're ready to solve:

$$(J + 8) = 2(B + 8) \rightarrow J + 8 = 2B + 16$$ Simplify grouped terms.
$$J = B + 13 \rightarrow J - 13 = B$$ Isolate the variable you want to eliminate.
$$J + 8 = 2(J - 13) + 16$$ Substitute into the other equation.
$$J + 8 = 2J - 26 + 16$$ Simplify grouped terms.

$$
\begin{array}{r}
J + 8 = 2J - 10 \\
\underline{-J + 10 \quad -J + 10} \\
18 = J
\end{array}
$$

The question asks for Jack's age, so you have your answer. Now you can review what you know about Word Problems and the steps to take to solve them:

Step 1: Identify unknowns and create variables.

- Don't forget to use descriptive letters (e.g., shorter piece = S).

- Be *very specific* when dealing with questions that contain two distinct but related situations (e.g., Jack's age *now* = J vs. Jack's age in 8 years = $J + 8$).

Step 2: Identify relationships and create equations.

- Once you have identified how many unknowns (variables) you have, try to find the same number of equations in the text, because you will usually need the same number of equations as you have variables. However, you need to be on the lookout for questions that ask about variable combinations, such as xy or $x + y$, resulting in the need for fewer equations than the number of variables.

- Don't forget to look at one piece of the question at a time. Don't try to do everything at once!

- Use numbers to check that you have set up your equation correctly. For example, if it says that Jack is twice as old as Ben, which is correct: $J = 2B$ or $2J = B$? If Jack were 40, Ben would be 20, so $40 = 2(20)$ or $2(40) = 20$?

Step 3: Identify what the question is asking for.

- Having a clear goal can prevent you from losing track of what you're doing and can help you stay focused on the task at hand. By the way, steps 1–3 can happen in any order you want.

Step 4: Solve for the *wanted* element (often by using substitution).

- The ability to perform every step accurately and efficiently is critical to success on the GRE. Make sure to **answer the right question**. A good habit is to write on your paper—before you begin calculating—what the final question is asking. For instance, if the question asks for Mary's age in 5 years, write "$M + 5$?" on your paper and circle it.

Now that you've gone through the basic steps, it's time to practice translating Word Problems into equations. But first, here are some common mathematical relationships found on the GRE, words and phrases you might find used to describe them, and their translations. Use them to help you with the drill sets at the end of this chapter.

Common Word Problem Phrases

Addition

Add, Sum, Total (of parts), More Than: +

The sum of x and y: $x + y$

The sum of the three funds combined: $a + b + c$

When fifty is added to his age: $a + 50$

Six pounds heavier than Dave: $D + 6$

A group of men and women: $m + w$

The cost is marked up: $c + m$

Subtraction

Minus, Difference, Less Than: −

x minus five: $x - 5$

The difference between Quentin's and Rachel's heights (if Quentin is taller): $Q - R$

Four pounds less than expected: $e - 4$

The profit is the revenue minus the cost: $P = R - C$

Multiplication

The product of h and k: $h \times k$

The number of reds times the number of blues: $r \times b$

One-fifth of y: $(1/5) \times y$

n persons have x beads each: total number of beads $= nx$

Go z miles per hour for t hours: distance $= zt$ miles

Ratios and Division

Quotient, Per, Ratio, Proportion: ÷ or /

Five dollars every two weeks: (5 dollars/2 weeks) → 2.5 dollars a week

The ratio of x to y: x/y

The proportion of girls to boys: g/b

Average or Mean (sum of terms divided by the total number of terms)

The average of a and b: $\dfrac{a+b}{2}$

The average salary of the three doctors: $\dfrac{x+y+z}{3}$

A student's average score on 5 tests was 87: $\dfrac{\text{sum}}{5} = 87$ or $\dfrac{a+b+c+d+e}{5} = 87$

Translating Words Correctly

1. **Avoid writing relationships backwards.**

If You See…	Write:			Not:	
"*A* is half the size of *B*."	✓	$A = \dfrac{1}{2}B$	✗	$B = \dfrac{1}{2}A$	
"*A* is 5 less than *B*."	✓	$A = B - 5$	✗	$A = 5 - B$	
"*A* is less than *B*."	✓	$A < B$	✗	$A > B$	
"Jane bought twice as many apples as bananas."	✓	$A = 2B$	✗	$2A = B$	

2. **Quickly check your translation with easy numbers.**

For the last example above, you might think the following:

> "Jane bought twice as many apples as bananas. More apples than bananas. Say she buys 5 bananas. She buys twice as many apples—that's 10 apples. Makes sense. So the equation is Apples equals 2 times Bananas, or $A = 2B$, not the other way around."

These numbers do not have to satisfy any other conditions of the problem. Use these "quick picks" only to test the form of your translation.

3. **Write an unknown percent as a variable divided by 100.**

If You See…	Write			Not	
"*P* is *X* percent of *Q*."	✓	$P = \dfrac{X}{100}Q$ or $\dfrac{P}{Q} = \dfrac{X}{100}$	✗	$P = X\%Q$	

(Cannot be manipulated.)

4. **Translate bulk discounts and similar relationships carefully.**

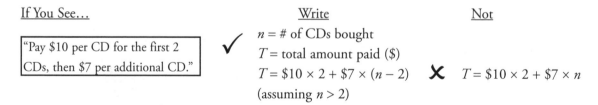

If You See…	Write	Not
"Pay \$10 per CD for the first 2 CDs, then \$7 per additional CD."	✓ n = # of CDs bought T = total amount paid (\$) $T = \$10 \times 2 + \$7 \times (n-2)$ (assuming $n > 2$)	✗ $T = \$10 \times 2 + \$7 \times n$

Always pay attention to the *meaning* of the sentence you are translating! If necessary, take a few extra seconds to make sure you've set up the algebra correctly.

Check Your Skills

Translate the following statements.

1. Lily is two years older than Melissa.

2. A small pizza costs $5 less than a large pizza.

3. Twice *A* is 5 more than *B*.

4. *R* is 45 percent of *Q*.

5. John has more than twice as many CDs as Ken.

Answers can be found on page 41.

Hidden Constraints

Notice that in some problems, there is a **hidden constraint** on the possible quantities. This would apply, for instance, to the number of apples and bananas that Jane bought. Since each fruit is a physical, countable object, you can only have a **whole number** of each type. Whole numbers are the integers 0, 1, 2, and so on. So you can have 1 apple, 2 apples, 3 apples, etc., and even 0 apples, but you cannot have fractional apples or negative apples.

As a result of this implied "whole number" constraint, you often have more information than you might think, and you might be able to answer a question with fewer facts.

Consider the following example:

> If Kelly received 1/3 more votes than Micah in a student election, which of the following could have been the total number of votes cast for the two candidates?
>
> (A) 12   (B) 13   (C) 14   (D) 15   (E) 16

Let M be the number of votes cast for Micah. Then Kelly received $M + (1/3)M$, or $(4/3)M$ votes. The total number of votes cast was therefore "votes for Micah" plus "votes for Kelly," or $M + (4/3)M$. This quantity equals $(7/3)M$, or $7M/3$.

Because M is a number of votes, it cannot be a fraction—specifically, not a fraction with a 7 in the denominator. Therefore, no matter what M is, the 7 in the expression $7M/3$ will not be cancelled out. As a result, the total number of votes cast must be a multiple of 7. Among the answer choices, the only multiple of 7 is 14, so the correct answer is (**C**).

Another way to solve this problem is this: the number of votes cast for Micah (M) must be a multiple of 3, since the total number of votes is a whole number. So $M = 3, 6, 9$, etc. Kelly received 1/3 more votes, so the number of votes she received is 4, 8, 12, etc. Thus, the total number of votes is 7, 14, 21, etc.

Not every unknown value related to "real-world" objects is restricted to whole numbers. Physical measurements such as weights, times, or speeds have to be positive numbers, but do not have to be integers.

A few physical measurements can even be negative (e.g., temperatures, *x*- or *y*-coordinates). Think about what is being measured or counted, and you will recognize whether a hidden constraint applies.

Check Your Skills

Translate the following statements.

2

6. In a certain word, the number of consonants is 1/4 more than the number of vowels. Which of the following is a possibility for the number of letters in the word?

    (A) 8   (B) 9   (C) 10   (D) 11   (E) 12

The answer can found on page 41.

Check Your Skills Answer Key

1. $L = M + 2$

2. $S = L - 5$

3. $2A = B + 5$

4. $R = \dfrac{45}{100} \times Q$ or $R = 0.45\,Q$

5. $J > 2K$

6. **(B):** There is a hidden constraint in this question. The number of vowels and the number of consonants must both be integers. The number of consonants is 1/4 more than the number of vowels, which means you need to multiply the number of vowels by 1/4 to determine how many more consonants there are. If you label the number of vowels v, then there are $v/4$ more consonants than vowels. The only way that $v/4$ will be an integer is if v is a multiple of 4.

If $v = 4$, there is 4/4 = 1 more consonant than there are vowels, so there are 4 + 1 = 5 consonants. That gives a total of 4 + 5 = 9 letters in the word. The correct answer is (B).

Problem Set

Solve the following problems using the four-step method outlined in this section.

1. Johan is 20 years older than Brian. 12 years ago, Johan was twice as old as Brian. How old is Brian?

2. Mrs. Miller has two dogs, Jackie and Stella, who weigh a total of 75 pounds. If Stella weighs 15 pounds less than twice Jackie's weight, how much does Stella weigh?

3. Caleb spends $72.50 on 50 hamburgers for the marching band. If single burgers cost $1.00 each and double burgers cost $1.50 each, how many double burgers did he buy?

4. United Telephone charges a base rate of $10.00 for service, plus an additional charge of $0.25 per minute. Atlantic Call charges a base rate of $12.00 for service, plus an additional charge of $0.20 per minute. For what number of minutes would the bills for each telephone company be the same?

5. Carla cuts a 70-inch piece of ribbon into 2 pieces. If the first piece is 5 inches more than one-fourth as long as the second piece, how long is the longer piece of ribbon?

6. Jayla started babysitting when she was 18 years old. Whenever she babysat for a child, that child was no more than half her age at the time. Jayla is currently 32 years old, and she stopped babysitting 10 years ago. What is the current age of the oldest person for whom Jayla could have babysat?

7. Ten years ago, Brian was twice as old as Aubrey.

Quantity A	**Quantity B**
Twice Aubrey's age today	Brian's age today

8. The length of a rectangular room is 8 feet greater than its width. The total area of the room is 240 square feet.

Quantity A	**Quantity B**
The width of the room in feet	12

9. Jaden earns a yearly base salary of $30,000, plus a commission of $500 on every car he sells above his monthly minimum of two cars. Last year, Jaden met or surpassed his minimum sales every month, and earned a total income (salary plus commission) of $60,000.

Quantity A	**Quantity B**
The number of cars Jaden sold last year	90

2

Solutions

1. **32 years old:**

Brian's age now = b
Johan's age now = j

Translate the first sentence:
(1) $j = b + 20$

Translate and simplify the second sentence:
(2) $(j - 12) = 2(b - 12)$
    $j - 12 = 2b - 24$
    $j = 2b - 12$

The problem says to solve for b, so combine the two equations by substituting the value for j in equation (1) into equation (2) to eliminate j and solve for b.

$b + 20 = 2b - 12$
$20 = b - 12$
$32 = b$

2. **45 pounds:** Let j = Jackie's weight, and let s = Stella's weight. Stella's weight is the Ultimate Unknown: $s = ?$

(1) The two dogs weigh a total of 75 pounds:

$j + s = 75$

(2) Stella weighs 15 pounds less than twice Jackie's weight:

$s = 2j - 15$

Combine the two equations by substituting the value for s from equation (2) into equation (1):

$j + (2j - 15) = 75$
$3j - 15 = 75$
$3j = 90$
$j = 30$

Find Stella's weight by substituting Jackie's weight into equation (1):

$30 + s = 75$
$s = 45$

3. **45 double burgers:**

Let s = the number of single burgers purchased.
Let d = the number of double burgers purchased.

(1) Caleb bought 50 burgers:
$s + d = 50$

(2) Caleb spent \$72.50 in all:
$s + 1.5d = 72.50$

Combine the two equations through substitution or by subtracting equation (1) from equation (2).

$$s + 1.5d = 72.50$$
$$\underline{- (s + \quad d = 50)}$$
$$0.5d = 22.5$$
$$d = 45$$

2

4. **40 minutes:**

Let x = the number of minutes.

A call made by United Telephone costs \$10.00 plus \$0.25 per minute: $10 + 0.25x$.

A call made by Atlantic Call costs \$12.00 plus \$0.20 per minute: $12 + 0.20x$.

Set the expressions equal to each other:

$$10 + 0.25x = 12 + 0.20x$$
$$0.05x = 2$$
$$x = \frac{2}{0.05} = \frac{200}{5} = 40$$

5. **52 inches:**

Let x = the 1st piece of ribbon.

Let y = the 2nd piece of ribbon.

(1) The ribbon is 70 inches long: (2) The 1st piece is 5 inches more than 1/4 as long as the 2nd:

$$x + y = 70$$ $$x = 5 + \frac{y}{4}$$

Combine the equations by substituting the value of x from equation (2) into equation (1):

$$5 + \frac{y}{4} + y = 70$$
$$20 + y + 4y = 280$$
$$5y = 260$$
$$y = 52$$

Now, since $x + y = 70$, $x = 18$. Thus, $x < y$, so y is the answer.

6. **23:** Since you are given actual ages for Jayla, the easiest way to solve the problem is to think about the extreme scenarios. At one extreme, 18-year-old Jayla could have babysat a child of age 9. Since Jayla is now 32, that child would now be 23. At the other extreme, 22-year-old Jane could have babysat a child of age 11. Since Jayla is now 32, that child would now be 21. You can see that the first scenario yields the oldest possible current age, 23, of a child that Jayla babysat.

7. **(A):** Let A and B denote Aubrey and Brian's ages today. Then, their ages 10 years ago would be given by $A - 10$ and $B - 10$, respectively. Those ages are related by the problem statement as:

$$B - 10 = 2(A - 10)$$

Expanding and simplifying yields:

$$B - 10 = 2A - 20$$
$$B = 2A - 10$$

MANHATTAN
PREP

Rewrite the quantities in terms of A and B. Twice Aubrey's age today is 2A and Brian's age today is B.

Ten years ago, Brian was twice as
old as Aubrey.

Quantity A	**Quantity B**
Twice Aubrey's age today = **2A**	Brian's age today = **B**

According to the equation, B is 10 less than 2A. Therefore, **Quantity A is greater**.

8. **(C):** Let L and W stand for the length and width of the room in feet. Then, from the first relation, you can write this equation:

(1) $L = W + 8$

Moreover, the area of a rectangle is given by length times width, such that:

(2) $LW = 240$

Taken together, you have two equations with two unknowns, and because the question involves the width rather than the length, you can eliminate the length by substituting from equation (1) into equation (2):

$(W + 8)W = 240$

Now expand the product and move everything to the left-hand side, so that you can solve the quadratic equation by factoring it. This gives:

$$W^2 + 8W = 240$$
$$W^2 + 8W - 240 = 0$$
$$(W + 20)(W - 12) = 0$$

The two solutions are $W = -20$ and $W = 12$. A negative width does not make sense, so W must equal 12 feet.

It is also possible to arrive at the answer by testing the value in Quantity B as the width of the room. Plug in 12 for W in equation (1):

$L = 12 + 8 = 20$ feet

If $W = 12$ and $L = 20$, then the area is (20)(12), which equals 240 square feet. Because this agrees with the given fact, you may conclude that 12 feet is indeed the width of the room.

Either method arrives at the conclusion. Therefore, **the two quantities are equal**.

9. **(B):** The simplest method for solving a problem like this is to work backwards from the value in Quantity B. Suppose Jaden sold exactly 90 cars. Then, since he met or surpassed his two car minimum each month (which adds up to 24 cars in the entire year), he would have sold another 90 − 24, which equals 66 cars above the minimum.

The commission he earned on those cars is calculated as follows:

$$\$500 \times 66 = \$33,000$$

This would put his total yearly income at \$30,000 (base salary) + \$33,000 (commission), which sums to \$63,000. However, you know that Jaden actually earned less than that; therefore, he must have sold fewer than 90 cars.

Quantity A	**Quantity B**
The number of cars Jaden sold last year = **less than 90**	90

Therefore, **Quantity B is greater**.

The alternative approach is to translate Jaden's total earnings into an algebraic expression. Suppose Jaden sold N cars. Once again, noting that he met or surpassed his monthly minimum sales, you would need to subtract 24 cars that do not contribute to his bonus from this total, and then solve for N as follows:

$$\$60,000 = \$30,000 + \$500 \times (N - 24)$$
$$\$30,000 = \$500 \times (N - 24)$$
$$60 = N - 24$$
$$84 = N$$

MANHATTAN
PREP

Chapter 3

of

Word Problems

Rates & Work

In This Chapter...

Chapter 3
Rates & Work

One common type of Word Problem (WP) on the GRE is the Rate problem. Rate problems come in a variety of forms on the GRE, but all are marked by three primary components: *rate*, *time*, and *distance* or *work*.

These three elements are related by the following equations:

> **Rate** × **Time** = **Distance**   OR
> **Rate** × **Time** = **Work**

These equations can be abbreviated as $RT = D$ or as $RT = W$. Basic Rate problems involve simple manipulation of these equations.

This chapter will discuss the ways in which the GRE makes rate situations more complicated. Often, $RT = D$ problems will involve more than one person or vehicle traveling. Similarly, many $RT = W$ problems will involve more than one worker.

The first step is to review some fundamental properties of Rate problems.

Basic Motion: The RTD Chart

All basic motion problems involve three elements: rate, time, and distance.

Rate is expressed as a ratio of distance and time, with two corresponding units. Some examples of rates include: 30 miles per hour, 10 meters/second, 15 kilometers/day, etc.

Time is expressed using a unit of time. Some examples of times include: 6 hours, 23 seconds, 5 months, etc.

Distance is expressed using a unit of distance. Some examples of distances include: 18 miles, 20 meters, 100 kilometers, etc.

You can make an "RTD chart" to solve a basic motion problem. Read the problem and fill in two of the variables. Then use the $RT = D$ formula to find the missing variable. For example:

If a car is traveling at 30 miles per hour, how long does it take to travel 75 miles?

An RTD chart is shown to the right. Fill in your RTD chart with the given information. Then solve for the time:

	Rate (miles/hr)	×	Time (hr)	=	Distance (miles)
Car	30 mi/hr	×		=	75 mi

$30t = 75$, or $t = 2.5$ hours

Matching Units in the RTD Chart

All the units in your RTD chart must match up with one another. The two units in the rate should match up with the unit of time and the unit of distance. For example:

It takes an elevator four seconds to go up one floor. How many floors will the elevator rise in two minutes?

The rate is 1 floor/4 seconds, which simplifies to 0.25 floors/second. Note: the rate is NOT 4 seconds per floor! This is an extremely frequent error. **Always express rates as "distance over time,"** not as "time over distance."

The time is 2 minutes. The distance is unknown.

Watch out! There is a problem with this RTD chart. The rate is expressed in floors per second, but the time is expressed in minutes. This will yield an incorrect answer.

	R (floors/sec)	×	T (min)	=	W (floors)
Elevator	0.25	×	2	=	?

To correct this table, change the time into seconds. Then all the units will match. To convert minutes to seconds, multiply 2 minutes by 60 seconds per minute, yielding 120 seconds.

	R (floors/sec)	×	T (sec)	=	D (floors)
Elevator	0.25	×	120	=	?

Once the time has been converted from 2 minutes to 120 seconds, the time unit will match the rate unit, and you can solve for the distance using the $RT = D$ equation:

$0.25(120) = d$ $d = 30$ floors

Another example:

> A train travels 90 kilometers/hour. How many hours does it take the train to travel 450,000 meters? (1 kilometer = 1,000 meters)

First, divide 450,000 meters by 1,000 to convert this distance to 450 km. By doing so, you match the distance unit (kilometers) with the rate unit (kilometers per hour).

	R $\times$	T $=$	D
	(km/hr)	(hr)	(km)
Train	90 $\times$	t $=$	450

You can now solve for the time: $90t = 450$. Thus, t is 5 hours. Note that this time is the "stopwatch" time: if you started a stopwatch at the start of the trip, what would the stopwatch read at the end of the trip? This is not what a clock on the wall would read, but if you take the *difference* of the start and end clock times (say, 1pm and 6pm), you will get the stopwatch time of 5 hours.

The RTD chart may seem like overkill for relatively simple problems such as these. In fact, for such problems, you can simply set up the equation $RT = D$ or $RT = W$ and then substitute. However, the RTD chart comes into its own when you have more complicated scenarios that contain more than one RTD relationship, as you'll see in the next section.

Check Your Skills

1. Convert 10 meters per second to meters per hour.

2. It takes an inlet pipe 2 minutes to supply 30 gallons of water to a pool. How many hours will it take to fill a 27,000 gallon pool that starts out empty?

Answers can be found on page 63.

Multiple Rates

Some rate questions on the GRE will involve *more than one trip or traveler*. To deal with this, you will need to deal with multiple $RT = D$ relationships. For example:

> Harvey runs a 30-mile course at a constant rate of 4 miles per hour. If Clyde runs the same track at a constant rate and completes the course in 90 fewer minutes, how fast did Clyde run?

An RTD chart for this question would have two rows: one for Harvey and one for Clyde.

	R $\times$	T $=$	D
	(miles/hr)	(hr)	(miles)
Harvey			
Clyde			

To answer these questions correctly, you need to pay attention to the relationships between these two equations. By doing so, you can reduce the total number of variables you need and can solve for the desired value with the number of equations you have.

For instance, both Harvey and Clyde ran the same course, so the distance they both ran was 30 miles. Additionally, you know Clyde ran for 90 fewer minutes. To make units match, you can convert 90 minutes to 1.5 hours. If Harvey ran t hours, then Clyde ran $(t - 1.5)$ hours:

	R × (miles/hr)	T = (hr)	D (miles)
Harvey	4	t	30
Clyde	r	$t - 1.5$	30

Now you can solve for t:

$$4t = 30$$
$$t = 7.5$$

If $t = 7.5$, then Clyde ran for $7.5 - 1.5 = 6$ hours. You can now solve for Clyde's rate. Let r equal Clyde's rate:

$$r \times 6 = 30$$
$$r = 5$$

For questions that involve multiple rates, remember to set up multiple $RT = D$ equations and look for relationships between the equations. These relationships will help you reduce the number of variables you need and allow you to solve for the desired value.

Relative Rates

Relative Rate problems are a subset of Multiple Rate Problems. The defining aspect of Relative Rate problems is that two bodies are traveling *at the same time*. There are three possible scenarios:

1. The bodies move towards each other.
2. The bodies move away from each other.
3. The bodies move in the same direction on the same path.

These questions can be dangerous because they can take a long time to solve using the conventional multiple rates strategy (discussed in the last section). You can save valuable time and energy by creating a third $RT = D$ equation for the rate at which the distance between the bodies changes:

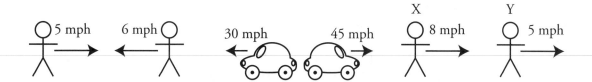

| Two people decrease the distance between themselves at a rate of 5 + 6 = 11 mph. | Two cars increase the distance between themselves at a rate of 30 + 45 = 75 mph. | Persons X and Y decrease the distance between themselves at a rate of 8 − 5 = 3 mph. |

3

> Imagine that two people are 14 miles apart and begin walking towards each other. Person A walks 3 miles per hour, and Person B walks 4 miles per hour. How long will it take them to reach each other?

To answer this question using multiple rates, you would need to make two important inferences: the time that each person walks is exactly the same (t hours) and the total distance they walk is 14 miles. If one person walks d miles, the other walks $(14 - d)$ miles. The chart would look like this:

	R (miles/hr)	×	T (hr)	=	D (miles)
Person A	3		t		d
Person B	4		t		14 − d

Alternatively, you can create an $RT = D$ equation for the rate at which they're getting closer to each other.

The rate at which they're getting closer to each other is 3 + 4 = 7 miles per hour. In other words, after every hour they walk, they are 7 miles closer to each other. Now you can create one $RT = D$ equation:

	R (miles/hr)	×	T (hr)	=	D (miles)
A + B	7		t		14

$$7t = 14$$
$$t = 2$$

You may very well have answered this question intuitively. But as the questions become more difficult, this method only becomes more valuable. Try this problem first on your own:

> Car X is 40 miles west of Car Y. Both cars are traveling east, and Car X is going 50% faster than Car Y. If both cars travel at a constant rate and it takes Car X 2 hours and 40 minutes to catch up to Car Y, how fast is Car Y going?

A multiple rates approach to this problem is difficult. Even if you do set up the equations, they will be difficult and time-consuming to solve. The multiple RTD chart would look like this:

	R (miles/hr)	×	T (hr)	=	D (miles)
Car X	1.5r		8/3		d
Car Y	r		8/3		d − 40

Instead, you can answer this question with one equation. If Car X is initially 40 miles behind Car Y, and they both travel until Car X catches up to Car Y, then the distance between them will have decreased by 40 miles. That is your distance. The distance between the two cars is decreasing at a rate of $1.5r − r = 0.5r$, and the time they travel is 8/3 hours:

$$0.5r \times \frac{8}{3} = 40$$

$$\frac{1}{2}r \times \frac{8}{3} = 40$$

$$\frac{4}{3}r = 40$$

$$r = 30$$

You defined the rate Car Y was traveling as r, so if $r = 30$, then Car Y was going 30 miles per hour.

For questions that involve relative rates, save yourself time and energy by creating an $RT = D$ equation for the rate at which the distance between the two bodies is changing.

Check Your Skills

3. One hour after Adrienne started walking the 60 miles from X to Y, James started walking from X to Y as well. Adrienne walks 3 miles per hour, and James walks 1 mile per hour faster than Adrienne. How far from X will James be when he catches up to Adrienne?

    (A) 8 miles   (B) 9 miles   (C) 10 miles   (D) 11 miles   (E) 12 miles

4. Nicky and Cristina are running a 1,000 meter race. Since Cristina is faster than Nicky, she gives him a 12-second head start. If Cristina runs at a pace of 5 meters per second and Nicky runs at a pace of only 3 meters per second, how many seconds will Nicky have run before Cristina catches up to him?

    (A) 15 seconds   (B) 18 seconds   (C) 25 seconds   (D) 30 seconds   (E) 45 seconds

Answers can be found on pages 63–64.

Average Rate: Don't Just Add and Divide

Consider the following problem:

> If Lucia walks to work at a rate of 4 miles per hour, but she walks home by the
> same route at a rate of 6 miles per hour, what is Lucia's average walking rate for
> the round trip?

It is very tempting to find an average rate as you would find any other average: add and divide. Thus, you might say that Lucia's average rate is 5 miles per hour (4 + 6 = 10 and 10 ÷ 2 = 5). However, this is INCORRECT!

If an object moves the **same distance** twice, but at **different rates**, then *the average rate will NEVER be the average of the two rates given for the two legs of the journey*. In fact, because the object spends *more time* traveling at the slower rate, *the average rate will be closer to the slower of the two rates than to the faster*.

In order to find the average rate, you must first find the *total* combined time for the trips and the *total* combined distance for the trips.

First, you need a value for the distance. Since all you need to know to determine the average rate is the *total time* and *total distance*, you can actually pick any number for the distance. The portion of the total distance represented by each part of the trip ("Going" and "Return") will dictate the time.

Pick a Smart Number for the distance. Since you would like to choose a multiple of the two rates in the problem, 4 and 6, 12 is an ideal choice.

Set up a Multiple RTD chart:

	Rate (mi/hr)	×	Time (hr)	_	Distance (mi)
Going	4	×	t	=	12
Return	6	×	t	=	12
Total	r	×	t	=	24

The times can be found using the *RTD* equation. For the Going trip, $4t = 12$, so t is 3 hours. For the Return trip, $6t = 12$, so t is 2 hours. Thus, the total time is 5 hours. Now plug in these numbers:

	Rate (mi/hr)	×	Time (hr)	=	Distance (mi)
Going	4	×	**3**	=	12
Return	6	×	**2**	=	12
Total	r	×	**5**	=	24

Now that you have the total time and the total distance, you can find the average rate using the RTD formula:

$$RT = D$$
$$r(5) = 24$$
$$r = 4.8 \text{ miles per hour}$$

Again, 4.8 miles per hour is *not* the simple average of 4 miles per hour and 6 miles per hour. In fact, it is the weighted average of the two rates, with the *times* as the weights. Because of that, the average rate is closer to the slower of the two rates.

You can test different numbers for the distance (try 24 or 36) to prove that you will get the same answer, regardless of the number you choose for the distance.

Check Your Skills

5. Juan bikes halfway to school at 9 miles per hour, and walks the rest of the distance at 3 miles per hour. What is Juan's average speed for the whole trip?

The answer can be found on page 64.

Basic Work Problems

Work problems are just another type of Rate problem. Instead of distances, however, these questions are concerned with the amount of "work" done.

Work takes the place of distance. Instead of $RT = D$, use the equation $RT = W$. The amount of work done is often a number of jobs completed or a number of items produced.

Time is the time spent working.

Rate expresses the amount of work done in a given amount of time.
Rearrange the equation to isolate the rate:

$$R = \frac{W}{T}$$

Be sure to express a rate as work per time (W/T), NOT time per work (T/W). For example, if a machine produces pencils at a constant rate of 120 pencils every 30 seconds, the rate at which the machine works is $\dfrac{120 \text{ pencils}}{30 \text{ seconds}} = 4$ pencils/second.

Many Work problems will require you to calculate a rate. Try the following problem:

Martha can paint $\dfrac{3}{7}$ of a room in $4\dfrac{1}{2}$ hours. If Martha finishes painting the room at the same rate, how long will it have taken Martha to paint the room?

(A) $8\dfrac{1}{3}$ hours (B) 9 hours (C) $9\dfrac{5}{7}$ hours (D) $10\dfrac{1}{2}$ hours (E) $11\dfrac{1}{7}$ hours

MANHATTAN
PREP

Your first step in this problem is to calculate the rate at which Martha paints the room. You can say that painting the entire room is completing 1 unit of work. Set up an *RTW* chart:

	R (rooms/hr)	×	T (hr)	=	W (rooms)
Martha	r		$\dfrac{9}{2}$		$\dfrac{3}{7}$

Now solve for the rate:

$$r \times \frac{9}{2} = \frac{3}{7}$$

$$r = \frac{3}{7} \times \frac{2}{9} = \frac{2}{21}$$

The division would be messy, so leave it as a fraction. Martha paints $\dfrac{2}{21}$ of the room every hour. Now you have what you need to answer the question. Remember, painting the whole room is the same as doing 1 unit of work. Set up another *RTW* chart:

	R (rooms/hr)	×	T (hr)	=	W (rooms)
Martha	$\dfrac{2}{21}$		t		1

Now solve for the time:

$$\left(\frac{2}{21}\right)t = 1$$

$$t = \frac{21}{2} = 10\frac{1}{2}$$

The correct answer is (D). Notice that the rate and the time in this case were reciprocals of each other. This will always be true when the amount of work done is 1 unit (because reciprocals are defined as having a product of 1).

Working Together: Add the Rates

More often than not, Work problems will involve more than one worker. When two or more workers are performing the same task, their rates can be added together. For instance, if Machine A can make 5 boxes in an hour, and Machine B can make 12 boxes in an hour, then working together the two machines can make 5 + 12 = 17 boxes per hour.

Likewise, if Lucas can complete 1/3 of a task in an hour and Serena can complete 1/2 of that task in an hour, then working together they can complete 1/3 + 1/2 = 5/6 of the task every hour.

If, on the other hand, one worker is undoing the work of the other, subtract the rates. For instance, if one hose is filling a pool at a rate of 3 gallons per minute, and another hose is draining the pool at a rate of 1 gallon per minute, the pool is being filled at a rate of 3 − 1 = 2 gallons per minute.

Try the following problem:

> Machine A fills soda bottles at a constant rate of 60 bottles every 12 minutes and Machine B fills soda bottles at a constant rate of 120 bottles every 8 minutes. How many bottles can both machines working together at their respective rates fill in 25 minutes?

3

To answer these questions quickly and accurately, it is a good idea to begin by expressing rates in equivalent units:

$$\text{Rate}_{\text{MachineA}} = \frac{60 \text{ bottles}}{12 \text{ minutes}} = 5 \text{ bottles/minute}$$

$$\text{Rate}_{\text{MachineB}} = \frac{120 \text{ bottles}}{8 \text{ minutes}} = 15 \text{ bottles/minute}$$

That means that working together they fill 5 + 15 = 20 bottles every minute. Now you can fill out an *RTW* chart. Let *b* be the number of bottles filled:

	R (bottles/min)	×	T (min)	=	W (bottles)
A + B	20		25		b

Now solve for the *b*:

$$b = 20 \times 25 = 500 \text{ bottles}$$

Remember that, even as Work problems become more complex, there are still only a few relevant relationships: $RT = W$ and $R_A + R_B = R_{A+B}$.

> Alejandro, working alone, can build a doghouse in 4 hours. Betty can build the same doghouse in 3 hours. If Betty and Carmelo, working together, can build the doghouse twice as fast as Alejandro, how long would it take Carmelo, working alone, to build the doghouse?

Begin by solving for the rate that each person works. Let *c* represent the number of hours it takes Carmelo to build the doghouse.

Alejandro can build $\frac{1}{4}$ of the doghouse every hour, Betty can build $\frac{1}{3}$ of the doghouse every hour, and Carmelo can build $\frac{1}{c}$ of the doghouse every hour.

MANHATTAN
PREP

The problem states that Betty and Carmelo, working together, can work twice as fast as Alejandro. That means that their rate is twice Alejandro's rate:

$$\text{Rate}_B + \text{Rate}_C = 2\left(\text{Rate}_A\right)$$
$$\frac{1}{3} + \frac{1}{c} = 2\left(\frac{1}{4}\right)$$
$$\frac{1}{c} = \frac{1}{2} - \frac{1}{3} = \frac{1}{6}$$
$$c = 6$$

It takes Carmelo 6 hours working by himself to build the doghouse.

When dealing with multiple rates, be sure to express rates in equivalent units. When the the work involves completing a task, remember to treat completing the task as doing one "unit" of work. Once you know the rates of every worker, add the rates of workers who work together on a task.

Check Your Skills

6. Sophie can address 20 envelopes in one hour. How long will it take her to address 50 envelopes?

7. If a steel mill can produce 1,500 feet of I-beams every 20 minutes, how many feet of I-beams can it produce in 50 minutes?

8. Tarik can complete a job in 12 minutes. If Andy helps Tarik, they can complete the job in 4 minutes. How long would it take for Andy to complete the job on his own?

Answers can be found on page 64–65.

Population Problems

The final type of Rate problem on the GRE is the Population problem. In such problems, some population typically increases *by a common factor* every time period. These can be solved with a Population chart.

Consider the following example:

> The population of a certain type of bacterium triples every 10 minutes. If the population of a colony 20 minutes ago was 100, in approximately how many minutes from now will the bacteria population reach 24,000?

You can solve simple Population problems, such as this one, by using a Population chart. Make a table with a few rows, labeling one of the middle rows as "NOW." Work forward, backward, or both (as necessary in the problem), obeying any conditions given in the problem statement about the rate of growth or decay. In this case, simply triple each population number as you move down a row. Notice that while the population increases by a constant *factor*, it does *not* increase by a constant *amount* each time period.

For this problem, the Population chart below shows that the bacterial population will reach 24,000 about 30 minutes from now.

In some cases, you might pick a Smart Number for a starting point in your Population chart. If you do so, pick a number that makes the computations as simple as possible.

Time Elapsed	Population
20 minutes ago	100
10 minutes ago	300
NOW	900
in 10 minutes	2,700
in 20 minutes	8,100
in 30 minutes	24,300

Check Your Skills

9. The population of amoebas in a colony doubles every two days. If there were 200 amoebas in the colony six days ago, how many amoebas will there be four days from now?

The answer can be found on page 65.

Check Your Skills Answer Key

1. **36,000 meters/hour:** First convert seconds to minutes. There are 60 seconds in a minute, so 10 m/sec × 60 sec/min = 600 m/min.

Now convert minutes to hours. There are 60 minutes in 1 hour, so 600 m/min × 60 min/hr = 36,000 m/hr.

2. **30 hours:** First simplify the rate: $R = \dfrac{30 \text{ gal}}{2 \text{ min}} = \dfrac{15 \text{ gal}}{1 \text{ min}}$, which is the same as 15 gal/min. The question

asks for the number of hours it will take to fill the pool, so convert minutes to hours. There are 60 minutes in an hour, so the rate is 15 gal/min × 60 = 900 gal/hr. Now you can set up an *RTW* chart. Let t be the time it takes to fill the pool:

	R (gal/hr)	×	T (hr)	=	W (gallons)
inlet pipe	900	×	t	=	27,000

Now solve for *t*:

$$900t = 27,000$$
$$t = 30 \text{ hours}$$

3. **12 miles:** Organize this information in an *RTD* chart as follows:

Set up algebraic equations to relate the information in the chart, using the $RT = D$ equation.

	R (mi/hr)	×	T (hr)	=	D (mi)
Adrienne	3	×	t + 1	=	d
James	4	×	t	=	d
Total	—		—		2d

Adrienne: $3(t + 1) = d$
James: $4t = d$

Substitute $4t$ for d in the first equation:

$$3(t + 1) = 4t$$
$$3t + 3 = 4t$$
$$t = 3$$

Therefore, $d = 4(3)$, which equals 12 miles.

Alternatively, you can model this problem as a "Chase." Adrienne has a 3-mile headstart on James (since Adrienne started walking 1 hour before James, and Adrienne's speed is 3 miles per hour). Since James is walking 1 mile per hour faster than Adrienne, it will take 3 hours for him to catch up to Adrienne.

Therefore, he will have walked (4 miles per hour)(3 hours) = 12 miles by the time he catches up to Adrienne.

4. **30 seconds:** This is a "Chase" problem in which the people are moving in the *same direction.*

Fill in the *RTD* chart. Note that Nicky starts 12 seconds before Cristina, so Nicky's time is $t + 12$.

	R (m/s)	×	T (second)	=	D (meter)
Cristina	5	×	t	=	$5t$
Nicky	3	×	$t + 12$	=	$3(t + 12)$

Write expressions for the total distance, and then set these two distances equal to each other.

Cristina: $5t$ = distance
Nicky: $3(t + 12)$ = distance
Combine: $5t = 3(t + 12)$
              $5t = 3t + 36$
              $2t = 36$
              $t = 18$

Therefore, Nicky will have run for 18 + 12 = 30 seconds before Cristina catches up to him.

5. **4.5 mph:** Assume a Smart Number for the distance to school. The Smart Number should be divisible by 9 and 3. The simplest choice is 18 miles for this distance. Now solve:

Time biking: $T = D/R = 9/9 = 1$ hr
Time walking: $T = D/R = 9/3 = 3$ hr
Total time: 1 hr + 3 hr = 4 hr

$$\text{average speed} = \frac{\text{total distance}}{\text{total time}} = \frac{18 \text{ miles}}{4 \text{ hours}} = 4.5 \text{ mph}$$

6. **2.5 hours:** If Sophie addresses 20 envelopes in 1 hour, then the rate at which she addresses is 20 envelopes/hr. Set up an *RTW* equation:

20 envelopes/hr × T = 50 envelopes
T = 50/20 = 2.5 hr

7. **3,750 feet:** The rate at which the steel mill produces I-beams is $\dfrac{1,500 \text{ ft}}{20 \text{ min}} = 75$ ft/min. Next, set up an *RTW* equation. Let w represent the number of feet of I-beam produced:

75 ft/min × 50 min = w
3,750 ft = w

8. **6 minutes:** Always express work rates as jobs per unit of time. Remember that the combined rates for Tarik and Andy are additive:

$$\underbrace{\frac{1 \text{ job}}{12 \text{ minutes}}}_{\text{Tarik}} + \underbrace{\frac{1 \text{ job}}{a \text{ minutes}}}_{\text{Andy}} = \frac{1 \text{ job}}{4 \text{ minutes}}$$

$$\frac{1}{12} + \frac{1}{a} = \frac{1}{4}$$

$$\frac{1}{a} = \frac{1}{4} - \frac{1}{12}$$

$$\frac{1}{a} = \frac{3}{12} - \frac{1}{12} = \frac{1}{6} \qquad a = 6 \text{ minutes}$$

9. **6,400:**

Time	Population
6 days ago	200
4 days ago *(Careful! Count by two days.)*	400
2 days ago	800
NOW	1,600
2 days from now	3,200
4 days from now	6,400

Problem Set

Solve the following problems using the strategies you have learned in this section. Use *RTD* or *RTW* charts as appropriate to organize information.

1. A cat travels at a speed of 60 inches/second. How long will it take this cat to travel 300 feet? (12 inches = 1 foot)

2. Water is being poured into a tank at the rate of approximately 4 cubic feet per hour. If the tank is 6 feet long, 4 feet wide, and 8 feet deep, how many hours will it take to fill up the tank?

3. The population of grasshoppers doubles in a particular field every year. Approximately, how many years will it take the population to grow from 2,000 grasshoppers to 1,000,000 or more?

4. An empty bucket being filled with paint at a constant rate takes 6 minutes to be filled to 7/10 of its capacity. How much more time will it take to fill the bucket to full capacity?

5. Four years from now, the population of a colony of bees will reach 1.6×10^8. If the population of the colony doubles every 2 years, what was the population 4 years ago?

6. The Technotronic can produce 5 bad songs per hour. Wanting to produce bad songs more quickly, the record label also buys a Wonder Wheel, which works as fast as the Technotronic. Working together, how many bad songs can the two produce in 72 minutes?

7. Jack is putting together gift boxes at a rate of 3 per hour in the first hour. Then Jill comes over and yells, "Work faster!" Jack, now nervous, works at the rate of only 2 gift boxes per hour for the next 2 hours. Then Alexandra comes to Jack and whispers, "The steadiest hand is capable of the divine." Jack, calmer, then puts together 5 gift boxes in the fourth hour. What is the average rate at which Jack puts together gift boxes over the entire period?

8. A bullet train leaves Kyoto for Tokyo traveling 240 miles per hour at 12 noon. Ten minutes later, a train leaves Tokyo for Kyoto traveling 160 miles per hour. If Tokyo and Kyoto are 300 miles apart, at what time will the trains pass each other?

    (A) 12:40pm   (B) 12:49pm   (C) 12:55pm   (D) 1:00pm   (E) 1:05pm

9. Andrew drove from A to B at 60 miles per hour. Then he realized that he forgot something at A, and drove back at 80 miles per hour. He then zipped back to B at 90 mph. What was his approximate average speed in miles per hour for the entire trip?

10. A car travels from Town A to Town B at an average speed of 40 miles per hour, and returns immediately along the same route at an average speed of 50 miles per hour. What is the average speed in miles per hour for the round-trip?

11. Two hoses are pouring water into an empty pool. Hose 1 alone would fill up the pool in 6 hours. Hose 2 alone would fill up the pool in 4 hours. How long would it take for both hoses to fill up two-thirds of the pool?

3

12. Aimee takes 6 minutes to pack a box and Brianna takes 5 minutes to pack a box. How many hours will it take them to pack 110 boxes?

13. Hector can solve one word problem every 4 minutes before noon, and one word problem every 10 minutes after noon.

Quantity A	**Quantity B**
The number of word problems Hector can solve between 11:40am and noon	The number of word problems Hector can solve between noon and 12:40pm

14. The number of users (non-zero) of a social networking website doubles every 4 months.

Quantity A	**Quantity B**
Ten times the number of users one year ago	The number of users today

15. A bullet train can cover the 420 kilometers between Xenia and York at a rate of 240 kilometers per hour.

Quantity A	**Quantity B**
The number of minutes it will take the train to travel from Xenia to York	110

Solutions

1. **1 minute:** This is a simple application of the $RT = D$ formula, involving one unit conversion. First convert the rate, 60 inches/second, into 5 feet/second (given that 12 inches = 1 foot). Substitute this value for R. Substitute the distance, 300 feet, for D. Then solve:

	R (ft/sec)	×	T (sec)	=	D (ft)
	5	×	t	=	300

$$(5 \text{ ft/s})(t) = 300 \text{ ft}$$

$$t = \frac{300 \text{ ft}}{5 \text{ ft/s}} = 60 \text{ seconds} = 1 \text{ minute}$$

2. **48 hours:** The capacity of the tank is $6 \times 4 \times 8$, or 192 cubic feet. Use the $RT = W$ equation, substituting the rate, 4 ft³/hour, for R, and the capacity, 192 cubic feet, for W:

	R (ft³/hr)	×	T (hr)	=	W (ft)
	4	×	t	=	192

$$(4 \text{ cubic feet/hr})(t) = 192 \text{ cubic feet}$$

$$t = \frac{192 \text{ cubic feet}}{4 \text{ cubic feet/hr}} = 48 \text{ hours}$$

3. **9 years:** Organize the information given in a population chart. Notice that since the population is increasing exponentially, it does not take very long for the population to top 1,000,000.

Time Elapsed	Population
NOW	2,000
1 year	4,000
2 years	8,000
3 years	16,000
4 years	32,000
5 years	64,000
6 years	128,000
7 years	256,000
8 years	512,000
9 years	1,024,000

4. **$2\frac{4}{7}$ minutes:** Use the $RT = W$ equation to solve for the rate, with $t = 6$ minutes and $w = 7/10$:

$$r(6 \text{ minutes}) = 7/10$$

$$r = \frac{7}{10} \div 6 = \frac{7}{10} \times \frac{1}{6} = \frac{7}{60} \text{ buckets per minute}$$

	R (bkt/min)	×	T (min)	=	W (bucket)
	r	×	6	=	7/ 10

Then, substitute this rate into the equation again, using 3/10 for w (the remaining work to be done):

$$\left(\frac{7}{60}\right) t = \frac{3}{10}$$

	R Regular	×	T Regular	=	W Regular
	7/60	×	t	=	3/10

$$t = \frac{3}{10} \div \frac{7}{60} = \frac{3}{10} \times \frac{60}{7} = \frac{18}{7} = 2\frac{4}{7} \text{ minutes}$$

5. 1×10^7: Organize the information given in a population chart.

Time Elapsed	Population
4 years ago	0.1×10^8
2 years ago	0.2×10^8
NOW	0.4×10^8
in 2 years	0.8×10^8
in 4 years	1.6×10^8

Then, convert:

$$0.1 \times 10^8 = 10,000,000 = 1 \times 10^7 \text{ bees}$$

6. **12 songs:** Since this is a "working together" problem, add the individual rates: $5 + 5 = 10$ songs per hour.

The two machines together can produce 10 bad songs in 1 hour. Convert the given time into hours:

$$(72 \text{ minutes})\left(\frac{1 \text{ hour}}{60 \text{ minutes}}\right) = \frac{72}{60} = 1.2 \text{ hours}$$

Then, use the $RT = W$ equation to find the total work done:

	R (songs/hr)	$\times$	T (hr)	$=$	W (songs)
	10	$\times$	1.2	$=$	w

$$(10)(1.2 \text{ hours}) = w$$
$$w = 12 \text{ bad songs}$$

7. **3 boxes per hour:** The average rate is equal to the total work done divided by the time in which the work was done. Remember that you cannot simply average the rates. You must find the total work and total time. The total time is 4 hours. To find the total work, add up the boxes Jack put together in each hour: $3 + 2 + 2 + 5 = 12$. Therefore, the average rate is $\frac{12}{4}$, or 3 boxes per hour. The completed chart is on the right:

	R (box/hr)	$\times$	T (hr)	$=$	W (box)
Phase 1	3	$\times$	1	$=$	3
Phase 2	2	$\times$	2	$=$	4
Phase 3	5	$\times$	1	$=$	5
Total	3 = 12/4		4 Sum		12 Sum

8. **12:49pm:** This is a "Kiss" problem in which the trains are moving towards each other.

Solve this problem by filling in the RTD chart. Note that the train going from Kyoto to Tokyo leaves first, so its time is longer by 10 minutes, which is 1/6 hour.

	R (mi/hr)	$\times$	T (hr)	$=$	D (mi)
Train K to T	240	$\times$	$t + 1/6$	$=$	$240(t + 1/6)$
Train T to K	160	$\times$	t	$=$	$160t$
Total	—		—		300

Next, write the expressions for the distance that each train travels, in terms of t. Now, sum those distances and set that total equal to 300 miles:

$$240\left(t + \frac{1}{6}\right) + 160t = 300$$

MANHATTAN
PREP

$$240t + 40 + 160t = 300$$
$$400t = 260$$
$$20t = 13$$
$$t = \frac{13}{20} \text{ hour} = \frac{39}{60} \text{ hour} = 39 \text{ minutes}$$

The first train leaves at 12 noon. The second train leaves at 12:10pm. Thirty-nine minutes after the second train has left, at 12:49pm, the trains pass each other.

9. **Approximately 74.5 mph:** Use a Multiple *RTD* chart to solve this problem. Start by selecting a Smart Number for *d*, such as 720 miles. (This is a common multiple of the 3 rates in the problem.) Then work backwards to find the time for each trip and the total time:

$$t_A = \frac{720}{60} = 12 \text{ hrs}$$

$$t_B = \frac{720}{80} = 9 \text{ hrs}$$

$$t_C = \frac{720}{90} = 8 \text{ hrs}$$

$$t = 12 + 9 + 8 = 29 \text{ hours}$$

	R (mi/hr)	$\times$	T (hr)	$=$	D (mi)
A to B	60	$\times$	t_A	$=$	720
B to A	80	$\times$	t_B	$=$	720
A to B	90	$\times$	t_C	$=$	720
Total	—		t		2,160

$$\text{average speed} = \frac{\text{total distance}}{\text{total time}} = \frac{2{,}160}{29} \approx 74.5 \text{ miles per hour}$$

10. **$44\frac{4}{9}$ miles per hour:** Use a Multiple *RTD* chart to solve this problem. Start by selecting a Smart Number for *d*, such as 200 miles. (This is a common multiple of the two rates in the problem.) Then work backwards to find the time for each trip and the total time:

$$t_1 = \frac{200}{40} = 5 \text{ hrs} \qquad\qquad t_2 = \frac{200}{50} = 4 \text{ hrs} \qquad\qquad t = 4 + 5 = 9 \text{ hrs}$$

$$\text{average speed} = \frac{\text{total distance}}{\text{total time}} = \frac{400}{9} = 44\frac{4}{9} \text{ miles per hour}$$

Do NOT simply average 40 miles per hour and 50 miles per hour to get 45 miles per hour. The fact that the right answer is very close to this wrong result makes this error especially pernicious: avoid it!

11. **$1\frac{3}{5}$ hours:** If Hose 1 can fill the pool in 6 hours, its rate is 1/6 pool per hour, or the fraction of the job it can do in 1 hour. Likewise, if Hose 2 can fill the pool in 4 hours, its rate is 1/4 pool per hour. Therefore, the combined rate is 5/12 pool per hour (1/4 + 1/6 = 5/12).

$$RT = W$$
$$(5/12)t = 2/3$$
$$t = \frac{2}{\cancel{3}_1} \times \frac{\cancel{12}^4}{5} = \frac{8}{5} = 1\frac{3}{5}$$

	R (pool/hr)	$\times$	T (hr)	$=$	W (pool)
	5/12	$\times$	t	$=$	2/3

12. **5 hours:** Working together, Aimee and Brianna pack $\frac{1}{6} + \frac{1}{5} = \frac{11}{30}$ boxes per minute. Next use a proportion:

$$\frac{11 \text{ boxes}}{30 \text{ minutes}} = \frac{110 \text{ boxes}}{x \text{ minutes}}$$

$$x = \frac{(110)(30)}{(11)} = 300 \text{ minutes, or 5 hours}$$

13. **(A):** This problem can be solved using an *RTW* chart or by a proportion. There are 20 minutes between 11:40am and noon, and 40 minutes between noon and 12:40pm. Hector's work rate is different for the two time periods. For the work period before noon, this is the proportion:

Let *b* represent the number of problems Hector solves *before* noon:

$$\frac{b}{20 \, \text{min}} = \frac{1 \text{ problem}}{4 \text{ min}}$$
$$4b = 20$$
$$b = 5$$

Let *a* represent the number of problems Hector solves *after* noon:

$$\frac{a}{40 \text{ min}} = \frac{1 \text{ problem}}{10 \text{ min}}$$
$$10a = 40$$
$$a = 4$$

Rewrite the quantities:

Quantity A	**Quantity B**
The number of word problems Hector can solve between 11:40am and noon = 5	The number of word problems Hector can solve between noon and 12:40pm = 4

Therefore, **Quantity A is greater**.

14. **(A):** Set up a Population chart, letting X denote the number of users one year ago:

Time	Number of Users
12 months ago	X
8 months ago	$2X$
4 months ago	$4X$
NOW	$8X$

Ten times the number of users one year ago is $10X$, while the number of users today is $8X$. Rewrite the quantities:

Quantity A	**Quantity B**
Ten times the number of users one year ago = $10X$	The number of users today = $8X$

Therefore, $10X$ is greater than $8X$ because X must be a positive number. Thus, **Quantity A is greater**.

15. **(B):** You can use the rate equation to solve for the time it will take the train to cover the distance. Your answer will be in hours because the given rate is in kilometers per hour. Let t stand for the total time of the trip:

$$R \times T = D$$

$$(240) \times t = (420)$$

$$t = \frac{420}{240} = \frac{7}{4}$$

(Note that you can omit the units in your calculation if you verify ahead of time that you are dealing with a consistent system of units.) Finally, convert the time from hours into minutes:

$$\frac{7}{4} \times 60 = \frac{7}{\cancel{4}_{1}} \times \overset{15}{\cancel{60}} = 105 \text{ minutes}$$

Rewrite the quantities:

Quantity A	**Quantity B**
The number of minutes it will take the train to travel from Xenia to York	110

An efficient way to solve this problem is to use the value in Quantity B to "cheat." Assume the train traveled for 110 minutes. Convert 110 minutes to hours:

$$\frac{110}{60} = \frac{11}{6} \text{ hours}$$

Now multiply the time ($\frac{11}{6}$ hours) by the rate (240 kilometers per hour) to calculate the distance:

$$D = \frac{11}{6} \times 240 = \frac{11}{\cancel{6}_{1}} \times \overset{40}{\cancel{240}} = 440 \text{ kilometers}$$

The train can travel 440 kilometers in 110 minutes, but the distance between the cities is 420 kilometers. Therefore, the train must have traveled less than 110 minutes to reach its destination. Thus, **Quantity B is greater**.

Chapter 4 of Word Problems

Ratios

In This Chapter...

Chapter 4

Ratios

A ratio expresses a particular relationship between two or more quantities. Here are some examples of ratios:

> The two partners spend time working in the ratio of 1 to 3. (For every 1 hour the first partner works, the second partner works 3 hours.)

> Three sisters invest in a certain stock in the ratio of 2 to 3 to 8. (For every $2 the first sister invests, the second sister invests $3, and the third sister invests $8.)

> The ratio of men to women in the room is 3 to 4. (For every 3 men, there are 4 women.)

Here are some key points about ratios:

Ratios can be expressed in a few different ways:

1. Using the word "to", as in 3 to 4
2. Using a colon, as in 3 : 4
3. By writing a fraction, as in $\frac{3}{4}$ (note that this only works for ratios of exactly $\underline{2}$ quantities)

Ratios can express a part–part relationship or a part–whole relationship:

> A part–part relationship: The ratio of men to women in the office is 3 : 4.
> A part–whole relationship: There are 3 men for every 7 employees.

Notice that if there are only two parts in the whole, you can figure out a part–whole ratio from a part–part ratio, and vice versa.

The relationship that ratios express is division:

> If the ratio of men to women in the office is 3 : 4, then the number of men divided by the number of women equals $\frac{3}{4}$ or 0.75.

Remember that ratios only express a *relationship* between two or more items; they do not provide enough information, on their own, to determine the exact quantity for each item. For example, knowing that the ratio of men to women in an office is 3 to 4 does NOT tell you exactly how many men and

how many women are in the office. All you know is that the number of men is $\frac{3}{4}$ the number of

women. In addition to being tested in GRE Word Problems, this fact is also tested in Data Interpretation questions, which often contain charts that show part–part and part–whole ratios.

If two quantities have a constant ratio, they are directly proportional to each other. For example:

If the ratio of men to women in the office is 3 : 4, then $\frac{\#\text{ of men}}{\#\text{ of women}} = \frac{3}{4}$.

If the number of men is directly proportional to the number of women, then the number of men divided by the number of women is always the same. So if the ratio of men to women is 3 : 4, there could be 3 men and 4 women, 9 men and 12 women, or even 600 men and 800 women, but there could not be 4 men and 3 women because then the number of men divided by the number of women would NOT equal 3/4.

Label Each Part of the Ratio with Units

The order in which a ratio is given is vital. For example, "the ratio of dogs to cats is 2 : 3" is very different from "the ratio of dogs to cats is 3 : 2." The first ratio says that for every 2 dogs, there are 3 cats. The second ratio says that for every 3 dogs, there are 2 cats.

It is very easy to accidentally reverse the order of a ratio—especially on a timed test like the GRE. Therefore, to avoid these reversals, always write units on either the ratio itself or on the variables you create, or both.

Thus, if the ratio of dogs to cats is 2 : 3, you can write $\frac{x\,\text{dogs}}{y\,\text{cats}} = \frac{2\,\text{dogs}}{3\,\text{cats}}$, or simply $\frac{x\,\text{dogs}}{y\,\text{cats}} = \frac{2}{3}$, or even $\frac{D}{C} = \frac{2\,\text{dogs}}{3\,\text{cats}}$, where D and C are variables standing for the number of dogs and cats, respectively.

However, do not just write $\frac{x}{y} = \frac{2}{3}$. You could easily forget which variable stands for cats and which for dogs.

Also, NEVER write $\frac{2d}{3c}$. The reason is that you might think that d and c stand for *variables*—that is, numbers in their own right. Always write out the full unit.

Proportions

Simple Ratio problems can be solved with a proportion. For example:

> The ratio of girls to boys in the class is 4 to 7. If there are 35 boys in the class, how many girls are there?

Step 1: Set up a labeled proportion:

$$\frac{4 \text{ girls}}{7 \text{ boys}} = \frac{x \text{ girls}}{35 \text{ boys}}$$

Step 2: Cross-multiply to solve:

$$7x = 4 \times 35$$

$$x = \frac{4 \times 35}{7} = 20$$

Remember that you can cancel fractions to simplify calculations as you go ($35/7 = 5/1$), although you can usually avoid this extra step by using the calculator. For example:

$$\frac{4 \text{ girls}}{7 \text{ boys}} = \frac{x \text{ girls}}{35 \text{ boys}} \qquad \frac{4 \text{ girls}}{\cancel{7} \text{ 1 boy}} = \frac{x \text{ girls}}{\cancel{35} \text{ 5 boys}} \qquad \frac{4}{1} = \frac{x}{5} \qquad x = 20$$

Note: never cancel factors diagonally across an equals sign. That would change the values incorrectly.

Check Your Skills

1. The ratio of apples to oranges in a fruit basket is 3 : 5. If there are 15 apples, how many oranges are there?

2. Miki has 7 jazz CDs for every 12 classical CDs in his collection. If he has 60 classical CDs, how many jazz CDs does he have?

Answers can be found on page 83.

The Unknown Multiplier

For more complicated Ratio problems, in which the total of all items is given, the "Unknown Multiplier" technique is useful:

> The ratio of men to women in a room is 3 : 4. If there are 56 people in the room, how many of the people are men?

Using the methods from the previous page, you can write the ratio relationship as $\dfrac{M \text{ men}}{W \text{ women}} = \dfrac{3}{4}$.

Together with $M + W = 56$, you can solve for M (and W, for that matter). The standard algebra techniques used for solving this kind of "two equations and two unknowns" problem are substitution and elimination, which is noted in the Algebraic Translations chapter of this book.

However, there is even an easier way. It requires a slight shift in your thinking, but if you can make this shift, *you can save yourself a lot of work on some problems.* Instead of representing the number of men as M, represent it as $3x$, where x is some unknown (positive) number. Likewise, instead of representing the number of women as W, represent it as $4x$, where x is the same unknown number. In this case (as in many others), x has to be a whole number. This is another example of a *hidden constraint.*

What does this seemingly odd step accomplish? It guarantees that the ratio of men to women is 3 : 4.

The ratio of men to women can now be expressed as $\dfrac{3x}{4x}$, which reduces to $\dfrac{3}{4}$, the desired ratio. (Note that you can cancel the x's because you know that x is not zero.) This variable x is known as the **Unknown Multiplier**. The Unknown Multiplier allows you to reduce the number of variables, making the algebra easier.

Now determine the value of the Unknown Multiplier using the other equation:

$$\text{Men} + \text{Women} = 56$$

$$3x + 4x = 56$$

$$7x = 56$$

$$x = 8$$

Now you know that the value of x, the Unknown Multiplier, is 8. Therefore, you can determine the exact number of men and women in the room:

The number of men equals: $3x = 3(8) = 24$. The number of women equals: $4x = 4(8) = 32$.

When *should* you use the Unknown Multiplier? You should use it when (1) the *total* items is given, or (2) neither quantity in the ratio is already equal to a number or a variable expression. Generally, the first ratio in a problem can be set up with an Unknown Multiplier. In the "girls and boys" problem on the previous page, however, you can glance ahead and see that the number of boys is given as 35. This means that you can just set up a simple proportion to solve the problem.

The Unknown Multiplier is particularly useful with three-part ratios:

> A recipe calls for amounts of lemon juice, wine, and water in the ratio of 2 : 5 : 7. If all three combined yield 35 milliliters of liquid, how much wine was included?

Make a quick table:

Lemon Juice +	Wine +	Water =	Total
$2x$ +	$5x$ +	$7x$ =	$14x$

Now solve for x: $14x = 35$, or $x = 2.5$. Thus, the amount of wine is $5x = 5(2.5) = 12.5$ milliliters.

In this problem, the Unknown Multiplier turns out not to be an integer. This result is fine, because the problem deals with continuous quantities (milliliters of liquids). In problems like the first one, which deals with integer quantities (men and women), the Unknown Multipier must be a positive integer. In that specific problem, the multiplier is literally the number of "complete sets" of 3 men and 4 women each.

You can only use the Unknown Multiplier only once per problem to solve though. So if the dogs to cats is 2 : 3 and cats to mice is 5 : 4, you shouldn't write $2x : 3x$ and $5y : 4y$. Instead, you need to make a common term.

Check Your Skills

3. The ratio of apples to oranges in a fruit basket is 3 : 5. If there are a total of 48 pieces of fruit, how many oranges are there?

4. Steve has nuts, bolts, and washers in the ratio 5 : 4 : 6. If he has a total of 180 pieces of hardware, how many bolts does he have?

5. A dry mixture consists of 3 cups of flour for every 2 cups of sugar. How much sugar is in 4 cups of the mixture?

The answers can be found on pages 83–84.

Multiple Ratios: Make a Common Term

You may encounter two ratios containing a common element. To combine the ratios, you can use a process similar to creating a common denominator for fractions.

Because ratios act like fractions, you can multiply both sides of a ratio (or all sides, if there are more than two) by the same number, just as you can multiply the numerator and denominator of a fraction by the same number. You can change *fractions* to have common *denominators*. Likewise, you can change *ratios* to have common *terms* corresponding to the same quantity. Consider the following problem:

In a box containing action figures of the three Fates from Greek mythology, there are 3 figures of Clotho for every 2 figures of Atropos, and 5 figures of Clotho for every 4 figures of Lachesis.

(a)   What is the least number of action figures that could be in the box?

(b)   What is the ratio of Lachesis figures to Atropos figures?

(a) In symbols, this problem tells you that $C : A = 3 : 2$ and $C : L = 5 : 4$. You cannot instantly combine these ratios into a single ratio of all three quantities, because the terms for C are different. However, you can fix that problem by multiplying each ratio by the right number, making both C's into the *least common multiple* of the current values:

C : A : L				C : A : L
3 : 2	→	Multiply by 5	→	15 : 10
5 : : 4	→	Multiply by 3	→	15 : : 12

This is the combined ratio: | 15: 10: 12 |

The actual *numbers* of action figures are these three numbers times an Unknown Multiplier, which must be a positive integer. Using the smallest possible multiplier, 1, there are $15 + 12 + 10 = 37$ action figures.

(b) Once you have combined the ratios, you can extract the numbers corresponding to the quantities in question and disregard the others: $L : A = 12 : 10$, which reduces to $6 : 5$.

Check Your Skills

6. A school has 3 freshmen for every 4 sophomores and 5 sophomores for every 4 juniors. If there are 240 juniors in the school, how many freshmen are there?

The answer can be found on page 84.

Check Your Skills Answer Key

1. **25:** Set up a proportion:

$$\frac{3\,\text{apples}}{5\,\text{oranges}} = \frac{15\,\text{apples}}{x\,\text{oranges}}$$

Now cross-multiply:

$$3x = 5 \times 15$$
$$3x = 75$$
$$x = 25$$

2. **35:** Set up a proportion:

$$\frac{7\,\text{jazz}}{12\,\text{classical}} = \frac{x\,\text{jazz}}{60\,\text{classical}}$$

Now cross-multiply:

$$12x = 7 \times 60$$
$$12x = 420$$
$$x = 35$$

3. **30:** Using the Unknown Multiplier, label the number of apples $3x$ and the number of oranges $5x$. Make a quick table:

Apples	+	Oranges	=	Total
$3x$	+	$5x$	=	$8x$

The total is equal to $8x$, and there are 48 total pieces of fruit, so:

$$8x = 48$$
$$x = 6$$

Therefore, oranges equal $5x = 5(6) = 30$.

4. **48:** Using the Unknown Multiplier, label the number of nuts $5x$, the number of bolts $4x$, and the number of washers $6x$. The total is $5x + 4x + 6x$:

$$5x + 4x + 6x = 180$$
$$15x = 180$$
$$x = 12$$

The total number of bolts is $4(12)$, which is 48.

5.   **8/5:** Using the Unknown Multiplier, label the amount of flour $3x$ and the amount of sugar $2x$. The total amount of mixture is $3x + 2x = 5x$:

$$5x = 4 \text{ cups}$$
$$x = 4/5$$

The total amount of sugar is $2(4/5)$, which equals 8/5 cups.

6.   **225:** Use a table to organize the different ratios:

F : S : J
3 : 4   3 freshmen for every 4 sophomores
    5 : 4   5 sophomores for every 4 juniors

Sophomores appear in both ratios, as 4 in the first and 5 in the second. The lowest common denominator of 4 and 5 is 20. Multiply the ratios accordingly:

F : S : J				F : S : J
3 : 4	→	Multiply by 5	→	15 : 20
5 : 4	→	Multiply by 4	→	20 : 16

The final ratio is F : S : J = 15 : 20 : 16. There are 240 juniors. Use a ratio to solve for the number of freshmen:

$$\frac{16}{240} = \frac{15}{x}$$

$$\frac{1}{15} = \frac{15}{x}$$

$$x = 225$$

Problem Set

Solve the following problems using the strategies you have learned in this section. Use proportions and the Unknown Multiplier to organize ratios.

For problems #1–5, assume that neither x nor y is equal to 0, to permit division by x and by y.

1. 48 : 2x is equivalent to 144 : 600. What is x?

2. x : 15 is equivalent to y to x. If $y = 3x$, what is x?

3. Brody's marbles have a red to yellow ratio of 2 : 1. If Brody has 22 red marbles, how many yellow marbles does Brody have?

4. Initially, the men and women in a room were in the ratio of 5 : 7. Six women leave the room. If there are 35 men in the room, how many women are left in the room?

5. It is currently raining cats and dogs in the ratio of 5 : 6. If there are 18 fewer cats than dogs, how many dogs are raining?

6. The amount of time that three people worked on a special project was in the ratio of 2 to 3 to 5. If the project took 110 hours, how many more hours did the hardest working person work than the person who worked the least?

7. A group of students and teachers take a field trip, such that the student to teacher ratio is 8 to 1. The total number of people on the field trip is between 60 and 70.

Quantity A	Quantity B
The number of teacher on the field trip	6

8. The ratio of men to women on a panel was 3 to 4 before one woman was replaced by a man.

Quantity A	Quantity B
The number of men on the panel	The number of women on the panel

9. A bracelet contains rubies, emeralds, and sapphires, such that there are 2 rubies for every 1
    emerald and 5 sapphires for every 3 rubies.

Quantity A	**Quantity B**
The minimum possible number of gemstones on the bracelet	20

4

Solutions

1. **100:** First set up a proportion and then cross-multiply:

$$\frac{48}{2x} = \frac{144}{600}$$

$$2x \times 144 = 48 \times 600$$

Isolate x and use the calculator to solve.

$$x = \frac{48 \times 600}{2 \times 144} = 100$$

2. **45:** First substitute $3x$ for y.

$$\frac{x}{15} = \frac{y}{x}$$

Then solve for x: $x = 3 \times 15 = 45$.

$$\frac{x}{15} = \frac{3x}{x} = 3$$

3. **11:** Write a proportion to solve this problem:

$$\frac{\text{red}}{\text{yellow}} = \frac{2}{1} = \frac{22}{x}$$

Cross-multiply to solve:

$$2x = 22$$
$$x = 11$$

4. **43:** First, establish the starting number of men and women with a proportion, and simplify:

$$\frac{5 \text{ men}}{7 \text{ women}} = \frac{35 \text{ men}}{x \text{ women}}$$

Cross-multiply:

$$5x = 7 \times 35$$

Isolate x and use the calculator to solve:

$$x = \frac{7 \times 35}{5} = 49$$

If 6 women leave the room, there are $49 - 6 = 43$ women left.

5. **108:** If the ratio of cats to dogs is 5 : 6, then there are $5x$ cats and $6x$ dogs (using the Unknown Multiplier). Express the fact that there are 18 fewer cats than dogs with an equation:

$$5x + 18 = 6x$$
$$x = 18$$

Therefore, there are $6(18) = 108$ dogs.

6. **33 hours:** Use an equation with the Unknown Multiplier to represent the total hours put in by the three people:

$$2x + 3x + 5x = 110$$
$$10x = 110$$
$$x = 11$$

Therefore, the hardest working person put in $5(11) = 55$ hours, and the person who worked the least put in $2(11) = 22$ hours. This represents a difference of $55 - 22 = 33$ hours.

7. **(A):** You can use an Unknown Multiplier x to help express the number of students and teachers. In light of the given ratio, there would be x teachers and $8x$ students, and the total number of people on the field trip would therefore be $x + 8x = 9x$. Note that x in this case must be a positive integer, because you cannot have fractional people.

The total number of people must therefore be a multiple of 9. The only multiple of 9 between 60 and 70 is 63. Therefore, x must be 63/9 which equals 7. Rewrite the quantities:

Quantity A	**Quantity B**
The number of teachers on the field trip = 7	6

Therefore, **Quantity A is greater**.

8. **(D):** While you know the ratio of men to women, you do not know the actual number of men and women. The following Before and After charts illustrate two of many possibilities:

Case 1	Men	Women
Before	3	4
After	4	3

Case 2	Men	Women
Before	9	12
After	10	11

These charts illustrate that the number of men may or may not be greater than the number of women after the move. Therefore, **the relationship cannot be determined from the information given.**

MANHATTAN
PREP

9. **(B):** This Multiple Ratio problem is complicated by the fact that the number of rubies is not consistent between the two given ratios, appearing as 2 in one and 3 in the other. You can use the least common multiple of 2 and 3 to make the number of rubies the same in both ratios:

$E : R : S$		$E : R : S$
1 : 2	multiply by 3	3 : 6
3 : 5	multiply by 2	6 : 10

Combining the two ratios into a single ratio yields:

$E : R : S :$ Total $= 3 : 6 : 10 : 19$

The smallest possible total number of gemstones is 19. Therefore, **Quantity B is greater**.

Chapter 5

of

Word Problems

Statistics

In This Chapter...

Chapter 5
Statistics

Averages

The **average** (or the **arithmetic mean**) of a list of numbers is given by the following formula (also known as "the average formula"):

$$\text{Average} = \frac{\text{Sum}}{\text{\# of terms}}, \text{ which is abbreviated as } A = \frac{S}{n}$$

The sum, S, refers to the sum of all the terms in the list.

The number, n, refers to the number of terms that are in the list.

The average, A, refers to the average value (arithmetic mean) of the terms in the list.

The language in an average problem will often refer to an "arithmetic mean." However, occasionally the concept is implied. "The cost per employee, if equally shared, is $20" means that the *average* cost per employee is $20.

A commonly used variation of the Average formula is:

$$\text{Average} \times \text{\# of terms} = \text{Sum, or } A \times n = S$$

This formula has the same basic form as the Rate × Time = Distance (RTD) equation that you reviewed in Chapter 3, so it lends itself readily to the same kind of table you would use for *RTD* problems.

Every GRE problem dealing with averages can be solved with the average formula. If you are asked to use or find the average of a list of numbers, you should not generally concentrate on the individual terms of the list. As you can see from the formulas above, all that matters is the *sum* of the terms—which often can be found even if the individual terms cannot be determined.

Using the Average Formula

The first thing to do for any GRE Average problem is to write down the average formula. Then, fill in any of the three variables (*S*, *n*, and *A*) that are given in the problem. For example:

The sum of 6 numbers is 90. What is the average term?

$$A = \frac{S}{n}$$

The sum, *S*, is given as 90. The number of terms, *n*, is given as 6. By plugging in, you can solve for the average: $\frac{90}{6} = 15$.

Notice that you do NOT need to know each term in the set to find the average!

Sometimes, using the average formula will be more involved. For example:

If the average of the list {2, 5, 5, 7, 8, 9, x} is 6.1, what is the value of x?

Plug the given information into the average formula, and solve for *x*:

$$(6.1)(7 \text{ terms}) = 2+5+5+7+8+9+x$$

$$A \times n = S \qquad\qquad 42.7 = 36 + x$$

$$6.7 = x$$

More complex average problems involve setting up two average formulas. For example:

Sam earned a $2,000 commission on a big sale, raising his average commission by $100. If Sam's new average commission is $900, how many sales has he made?

To keep track of two average formulas in the same problem, you can set up a Rate × Time = Distance (RTD)-style table. Instead of $RT = D$, Use $A \times n = S$, which has the same form. Sam's new average commission is $900, and this is $100 higher than his old average, so his old average was $800.

Note that the Number and Sum columns add up to give the new cumulative values, but the values in the Average column do *not* add up:

	Average	×	Number	=	Sum
Old total	800	×	n	=	800n
This sale	2,000	×	1	=	2,000
New total	900	×	$n+1$	=	900($n+1$)

The right-hand column gives the equation you need:

$$800n + 2000 = 900(n+1)$$
$$800n + 2000 = 900n + 900$$
$$1100 = 100n$$
$$11 = n$$

Remember: you are looking for the new number of sales, which is $n + 1$, so Sam has made a total of 12 sales.

Check Your Skills

1. The sum of 6 integers is 45. What is the average of the 6 integers?

2. The average price per item in a shopping basket is $2.40. If there are a total of 30 items in the basket, what is the total price of the items in the basket?

Answers can be found on page 103.

Evenly Spaced Sets: Take the Middle

You may recall that the average of a set of consecutive integers is the middle number (the middle number of *any* dataset is always its median—more on this later). This is true for any set in which the terms are spaced evenly apart. For example:

The average of the set {3, 5, 7, 9, 11} is the middle term 7, because all the terms in the set are spaced evenly apart (in this case, they are spaced 2 units apart).

The average of the set {12, 20, 28, 36, 44, 52, 60, 68, 76} is the middle term 44, because all the terms in the set are spaced evenly apart (in this case, they are spaced 8 units apart).

Note that if an evenly spaced set has two "middle" numbers, the average of the set is the average of these two middle numbers. For example:

The average of the set {5, 10, 15, 20, 25, 30} is 17.5, because this is the average of the two middle numbers: 15 and 20.

You do not have to write out each term of an evenly spaced set to find the middle number—the average term. All you need to do to find the middle number is to add the **first** and **last** terms and divide that sum by 2. For example:

The average of the set {101, 111, 121…581, 591, 601} is equal to 351, which is the sum of the first and last terms (101 + 601 = 702) divided by 2. This approach is especially attractive if the number of terms is large.

Check Your Skills

3. What is the average of the set {2, 5, 8, 11, 14}?

4. What is the average of the set {−1, 3, 7, 11, 15, 19, 23, 27}?

Answers can be found on page 103.

Weighted Averages

Properties of Weighted Averages

Although weighted averages differ from traditional averages, they are still averages, meaning that their values will still fall *between* the values being averaged (or between the highest and lowest of those values, if there are more than two).

A weighted average of only *two* values will fall closer to whichever value is weighted more heavily. For instance, if a drink is made by mixing 2 shots of a liquor containing 15% alcohol with 3 shots of a liquor containing 20% alcohol, then the alcohol content of the mixed drink will be closer to 20% than to 15%.

For example, take the weighted average of 20 and 30, with weights $\dfrac{a}{a+b}$ and $\dfrac{b}{a+b}$:

$$\text{Weighted average} = \frac{a}{a+b}(20) + \frac{b}{a+b}(30)$$

The weighted average will always be between 20 and 30, as long as a and b are both positive (and on the GRE, they always have been). A number line between 20 and 30 can help you visualize where the weighted average will fall:

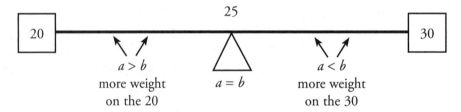

If, for example, you're told that the ratio of a to b is 3 to 1, then you know that the average will fall somewhere between 20 and 25, and you also know that it is possible to calculate the specific value:

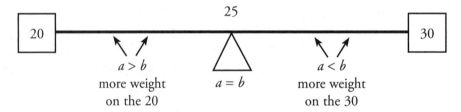

Check Your Skills

5. A stock portfolio is comprised of Stock A, whose annual gain was 10%, and Stock B, whose annual gain was 20%. If the stock portfolio gained 14% overall, does it contain more shares of Stock A or Stock B?

MANHATTAN
PREP

6. 2/3 of the aliens on Planet X are Zorgs, whose average IQ is 120. The rest are Weebs, whose average IQ is 180. What is the average IQ of all the aliens on Planet X?

Answers can be found on page 103.

Median: The Middle Number

Some GRE problems feature a second type of average: the *median*, or "middle value." The median is calculated in one of two ways, depending on the number of data points in the set.

For lists containing an **odd** number of values, the median is the ***unique middle value*** when the data are arranged in increasing (or decreasing) order.

For lists containing an **even** number of values, the median is the ***average (arithmetic mean) of the two middle values*** when the data are arranged in increasing (or decreasing) order.

Note on terminology: the GRE is very precise in its use of mathematical terms. If a question refers to a group of numbers as a *set*, you know that all of the numbers are different from each other; because the mathematical definition of a *set* says that there can't be any repeat values. However, if a question refers to a group of numbers as a *list*, repeat values are allowed, but not required. So {3, 4, 9, 17} is a *set* and a *list*, but {3, 4, 9, 9}, is just a *list*. You can find the median of any *list* or *set* of numbers though. You can also find the median of a *dataset* (or *data set*), which despite having the word *set* in its name, is actually just a large list in the language of math.

The median of the set {5, 17, 24, 25, 28} is the unique middle number, 24. The median of the list {3, 4, 9, 17} is the mean of the two middle values (4 and 9), or 6.5. Notice that the median of a list containing an *odd* number of values must be a value in the set. However, the median of a list containing an *even* number of values does not have to be in the list—and indeed *will not be*, unless the two middle values are equal.

Medians of Lists Containing Unknown Values

Unlike the arithmetic mean, the median of a set depends only on the one or two values in the middle of the ordered set. Therefore, you may be able to determine a specific value for the median of a set *even if one or more unknowns are present.*

For instance, consider the unordered list {x, 2, 5, 11, 11, 12, 33}. No matter whether x is less than 11, equal to 11, or greater than 11, the median of the resulting set will be 11. (Try substituting different values of x to see that the median does not change.)

By contrast, the median of the unordered list {x, 2, 5, 11, 12, 12, 33} depends on x. If x is 11 or less, the median is 11. If x is between 11 and 12, the median is x. Finally, if x is 12 or more, the median is 12.

<u>Check Your Skills</u>

7. What is the median of the set {6, 2, −1, 4, 0}?

8. What is the median of the set {1, 2, *x*, 8}, if 2 < *x* < 8?

Answers can be found on page 103.

Standard Deviation

The mean and median both give "average" or "representative" values for a list, but they do not tell the whole story. It is possible for two lists to have the same average but to differ widely in how spread out their values are. To describe the spread, or variation, of the data in a list, use a different measure: the **standard deviation**.

Standard deviation (SD) indicates how far from the average (mean) the data points typically fall. Therefore:

- A small SD indicates that a list is clustered closely around the average (mean) value.

- A large SD indicates that the list is spread out widely, with some points appearing far from the mean.

Consider the lists {5, 5, 5, 5}, {2, 4, 6, 8}, and {0, 0, 10, 10}. These lists all have the same mean value of 5. You can see at a glance, though, that the lists are very different, and the differences are reflected in their SDs. The first list has an SD of zero (no spread at all), the second list has a moderate SD, and the third list has a large SD.

The formula for calculating SD is rather cumbersome. The good news is that you do not need to know this formula because **it is very unlikely that a GRE problem will ask you to calculate an exact SD**. If you just pay attention to what the average spread is doing, you should be able to answer all GRE SD problems, which involve either (1) changes in the SD when a list is transformed, or (2) comparisons of the SDs of two or more lists. Just remember that the more spread out the numbers, the greater the SD.

If you see a problem focusing on changes in the SD, ask yourself whether the changes move the data closer to the mean, farther from the mean, or neither. If you see a problem requiring comparisons, ask yourself which list is more spread out from its mean.

You should also know the term variance, which is just the *square* of the standard deviation.

Following are some sample problems to help illustrate SD properties:

(a)   Which list has the greater standard deviation: {1, 2, 3, 4, 5} or {440, 442, 443, 444, 445}?

(b)   If each data point in a list is increased by 7, does the list's standard deviation increase, decrease, or remain constant?

(c)   If each data point in a list is increased by a factor of 7, does the list's SD increase, decrease, or remain constant?

In (a), the second list has the greater SD. One way to understand this is to observe that the gaps between its numbers are, on average, slightly bigger than the gaps in the first list (because the first two numbers are 2 units apart). Another way to resolve the issue is to observe that the list {441, 442, 443, 444, 445} would have the same standard deviation as {1, 2, 3, 4, 5}. Replacing 441 with 440, which is farther from the mean, will increase the SD.

In any case, only the *spread* matters. The numbers in the second list are much more "consistent" in some sense—they are all within about 1% of each other, while the largest numbers in the first list are several times the smallest ones. However, this "percent variation" idea is irrelevant to the SD.

In (b), the SD will not change. "Increased by 7" means that the number 7 is *added* to each data point in the list. This transformation will not affect any of the gaps between the data points, and thus it will not affect how far the data points are from the mean. If the list were plotted on a number line, this transformation would merely slide the points 7 units to the right, taking all the gaps, and the mean, along with them.

In (c), the SD will increase. "Increased by a *factor* of 7" means that each data point is multiplied by 7. This transformation will make all the gaps between points 7 times as big as they originally were. Thus, each point will fall 7 times as far from the mean. The SD will increase by a factor of 7.

Check Your Skills

9. Which list has a greater standard deviation?

    List A: {3, 4, 5, 6, 7}   List B: {3, 3, 5, 7, 7}

The answer can be found on page 104.

Range

The range of a list of numbers is another measure of the dispersion of the list of numbers. It is defined simply as the difference between the largest number in the list and the smallest number in the list. For example, in the list {3, 6, −1, 4, 12, 8}, the largest number is 12 and the smallest number is −1. Therefore, the range is 12 − (−1) = 13.

Check Your Skills

10. The list {2, −1, x, 5, 3} has a range of 13. What are the possible values for x?

The answer can be found on page 104.

Quartiles and Percentiles

Lists of numbers can be described by Quartiles, and for larger datasets (remember that a dataset is just another word for a list), by Percentiles. For example, consider the following dataset of 16 numbers:

$$\left\{ \underbrace{0, 1, 2, 2}_{\text{Quartile 1}} \;\middle|\; \underbrace{3, 4, 5, 5}_{\text{Quartile 2}} \;\middle|\; \underbrace{5, 6, 7, 8}_{\text{Quartile 3}} \;\middle|\; \underbrace{10, 11, 13, 14}_{\text{Quartile 4}} \right\}$$

$$Q_1 \qquad\qquad Q_2 \qquad\qquad Q_3$$

The list is divided into four quartiles, each divided with "Quartile Markers." Q_1 is the average of the highest item in Quartile 1 and the lowest item in Quartile 2, and so on. Thus, $Q_1 = \dfrac{2+3}{2} = 2.5$, $Q_2 = \dfrac{5+5}{2} = 5$, and $Q_3 = \dfrac{8+10}{2} = 9$. Thus, Q_2 is *the same as* the median of the list.

For a larger dataset (of, say, 1,000 numbers), Percentiles can be used. Thus, in a dataset of 1,000 numbers, the 10 smallest items will be in Percentile 1, and P_1 will be the average of the 10th and 11th smallest items. Note that $P_{25} = Q_1$, $P_{50} = Q_2 = $ median, and $P_{75} = Q_3$.

Check Your Skills

11. In the list {2, 3, 0, 8, 11, 1, 4, 7, 8, 2, 1, 3}, what is $Q_3 - Q_1$?

The answer can be found on page 104.

The Normal Distribution

One of the most important distributions for random variables is the Normal Distribution (also known as the Gaussian Distribution). The Normal Distribution looks like the classic "bell curve," rounded in the middle with long tails, and symmetric around the mean (which equals the median).

Normal Distribution with Mean = 10 and Standard Deviation = 4

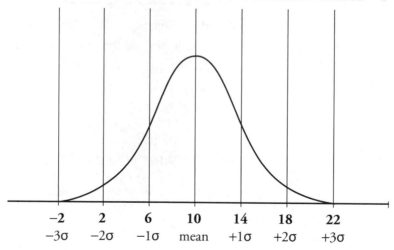

The GRE tests on distributions that are both *normal* and *approximately normal*. These distributions have the following characteristics:

- The *mean* and *median* are **equal**, or *almost exactly* equal.

- The data is exactly, or *almost exactly*, symmetric around the mean/median.

- Roughly 2/3 of the sample will fall within 1 standard deviation of the mean. That means that roughly 1/3 of the sample falls within 1 standard deviation below the mean and roughly 1/3 of the sample falls within 1 standard deviation above the mean. Thus, in the example above, a value of 6 is at roughly $50\% - \left(\frac{1}{2}\right)\left(\frac{2}{3}\right) = 17\%$, or the 17th Percentile. A value of 14 is at roughly $50\% + \left(\frac{1}{2}\right)\left(\frac{2}{3}\right) = 83\%$, or the 83rd Percentile.

- Roughly 96% of the sample will fall within 2 standard deviations of the mean. In other words, roughly 48% of the sample falls between the mean and 2 standard deviations below the mean; roughly 48% of the sample falls between the mean and 2 standard deviations above the mean. Thus, in the example above, a value of 2 will be at $50\% - \left(\frac{1}{2}\right)(96\%) = 50\% - 48\% = 2\%$, or the 2nd Percentile. A value of 18 will be at $50\% + \left(\frac{1}{2}\right)(96\%) = 50\% + 48\% = 98\%$, or the 98th Percentile.

- Only about $\frac{1}{1,000}$ (0.1%) of the curve is 3 or more standard deviations below the mean; the same is true above the mean.

The GRE typically will only test these concepts in a general way, and it will not distinguish between random variables that are normally distributed versus ones that are *nearly* normally distributed. However, it is *important* to note that distributions that are *not* normal or nearly normal do *not* necessarily share the characteristics above. It is possible, for example, to construct distributions where the mean and median are substantially different, or where 100% of the observations fall within 2 standard deviations, or where more than 1% of the observations fall more than 3 standard deviations from the mean.

Check Your Skills

For questions #12–15, variable *X* is nearly normally distributed, with a mean of 6 and a standard deviation of 2.

12. Approximately what percent of the observations in *X* will be smaller than 4?

13. Approximately what percent of the observations in *X* will be greater than 12?

14. For variable *X*, approximately what percentile corresponds to a value of 2?

15. Would the answers to questions #12–14, be the same if variable *X* were <u>not</u> nearly normally distributed?

Answers can be found on page 104.

Check Your Skills Answer Key

1. **7.5:** $A = \dfrac{S}{n}$

$$A = \dfrac{45}{6} = 7.5$$

2. **\$72:** $A = \dfrac{S}{n}$

$$2.40 = \dfrac{S}{30}$$

$$S = 2.40(30) = 72$$

3. **8:** Notice that each term in the set is 3 more than the last. Because this set is evenly spaced, the median and the average will be the same. The median is 8, and so the average is also 8.

4. **13:** Notice that each term in the set is 4 more than the last. Because this set is evenly spaced, the median and the average will be the same. The number of terms in the set is even, so the median of the set is the average of the two middle terms: $A = \dfrac{(11+15)}{2} = 13$.

5. **Stock A:** Because the overall gain is closer to 10% than to 20%, the portfolio must be weighted more heavily towards Stock A, (i.e., contain more shares of Stock A).

6. **140:** 2/3 of the total population is Zorgs, and so the weight is 2/3. Similarly, the weight of the Weebs is 1/3. Now plug everything into the weighted average formula:

$$\text{Weighted Average} = \dfrac{2}{3}(120) + \dfrac{1}{3}(180)$$

$$= 80 + 60$$

$$= 140$$

7. **2:** First order the set from least to greatest:

$$\{6, 2, -1, 4, 0\} \rightarrow \{-1, 0, 2, 4, 6\}$$

The median is the middle number, which is 2.

8. $\dfrac{2+x}{2}$ **or** $1+\dfrac{x}{2}$**:** Because the number of terms is even, the median is the average of the two middle terms: $\dfrac{2+4}{2} = 3$. Since $2 < x < 8$, the lower of the two middle terms will be 2 and the higher of the two middle terms will be x. Therefore, the median is $\dfrac{2+x}{2}$, or simplified $1+\dfrac{x}{2}$.

5

9. **Dataset B:** Each dataset has a mean of 5, so the dataset whose numbers are further away from the mean will have the higher standard deviation. When comparing standard deviations, focus on the differences between each dataset. The numbers that each dataset has in common are highlighted:

Dataset A: {**3**, 4, **5**, 6, **7**}   Dataset B: {**3**, 3, **5**, 7, **7**}

Compare the numbers that are not the same. The numbers 4 and 6 in Dataset A are closer to the mean (5) than are the 3 and 7 in Dataset B. Therefore, the numbers in Dataset B are further away from the mean and Dataset B has a greater standard deviation.

10. **12 or −8:** If x is the smallest number, then 5 is the largest number in the list and $5 - x = 13$, so x is −8. If x is the largest number, then −1 is the smallest number in the list and $x - (-1) = 13$, so x is 12.

11. **6:** The first thing to do is to list these number elements in order, then determine the cutoff points for Q_1, Q_2, and Q_3:

$$\{0, 1, 1, \big| 2, 2, 3, \big| 3, 4, 7, \big| 8, 8, 11\}$$
$$Q_1 \quad Q_2 \quad Q_3$$

$$Q_3 = \frac{7+8}{2} = 7.5$$

$$Q_1 = \frac{1+2}{2} = 1.5$$

Therefore, $Q_3 - Q_1 = 6$.

12. **17%:** $50 - \left(\frac{1}{2}\right)\left(\frac{2}{3}\right) = 17\%$.

13. **Approximately 0.1%:** Roughly, 1 in 1,000 observations in a normal distribution will be 3 standard deviations above the mean. This is always true of a normal distribution: 96% of values fall within 2 standard deviations of the mean, leaving 2% of values to fall below and 2% of values to fall above.

14. **2nd Percentile:** Approximately $50\% - \left(\frac{1}{2}\right)(96\%) = 2\%$, or the 2nd Percentile.

15. **No, not necessarily.**

Problem Set

1. The average of 11 numbers is 10. When one number is eliminated, the average of the remaining numbers is 9.3. What is the eliminated number?

2. The average of 9, 11, and 16 is equal to the average of 21, 4.6, and what number?

3. For the list of numbers {4, 5, 5, 6, 7, 8, 21}, how much greater is the mean than the median?

4. The sum of 8 numbers is 168. If one of the numbers is 28, what is the average of the other 7 numbers?

5. If the average of the list {5, 6, 6, 8, 9, x, y} is 6, then what is the value of $x + y$?

6. On 4 sales, Matt received commissions of $300, $40, x, and $140. Without the x, his average commission would be $50 lower. What is x?

7. The class mean score on a test was 60, and the standard deviation was 15. If Elena's score was within 2 standard deviations of the mean, what is the lowest score she could have received?

8. Milo gets a $1,000 commission on a big sale. This commission alone raises his average commission by $150. If Milo's new average commission is $400, how many sales has Milo made?

9. Grace's average bowling score over the past 6 games is 150. If she wants to raise her average score by 10%, and she has two more games remaining in the season, what must her average score on the last two games be?

10. If the average of x and y is 50, and the average of y and z is 80, what is the value of $z - x$?

11. If $x > 0$ and the range of 1, 2, x, 5, and x^2 equals 7, what is the approximate average (mean) of the list?

12. Among the list {1, 2, 3, 4, 7, 7, 10, 10, 11, 14, 19, 19, 23, 24, 25, 26}, what is the ratio of the largest item in Quartile 2 to the average value in Quartile 4?

13. N is a normally distributed set with a mean of 0. If approximately 2% of the observations in N are −10 or smaller, what fraction of the observations are between 0 and 5?

14. A college class is attended by Poets and Bards in the ratio of 3 Poets for every 2 Bards. On a midterm, the average score of the Poets is 60 and the average score of the Bards is 80.

Quantity A	Quantity B
The overall average score for the class	70

15. $x > 2$

Quantity A	Quantity B
The median of $x - 4$, $x + 1$, and $4x$	The mean of $x - 4$, $x + 1$, and $4x$

16. *A* is the set of the first five positive odd integers. *B* is the set of the first five positive even integers.

Quantity A	Quantity B
The standard deviation of *A*	The standard deviation of *B*

5

Solutions

1. **17:** If the average of 11 numbers is 10, their sum is 11×10, which is 110. After one number is eliminated, the average is 9.3, so the sum of the 10 remaining numbers is 10×9.3, which is 93. The number eliminated is the difference between these sums: $110 - 93 = 17$.

2. **10.4:** $\dfrac{9+11+16}{3} = \dfrac{21+4.6+x}{3}$ $9 + 11 + 16 = 21 + 4.6 + x$ $x = 10.4$

3. **2:** The mean of the listed terms is the sum of the numbers divided by the number of terms: $56 \div 7 = 8$. The median is the middle number: 6. Thus, 8 is 2 greater than 6.

4. **20:** The sum of the other 7 numbers is 140 $(168 - 28)$. So, the average of the numbers is $140/7 = 20$.

5. **8:** If the average of seven terms is 6, then the sum of the terms is 7×6, which is 42. The listed terms have a sum of 34. Therefore, the remaining terms, x and y, must have a sum of $42 - 34$, which is 8.

6. **$360:** Without x, Matt's average sale is $(300 + 40 + 140) \div 3$, which is $160. With x, Matt's average is $50 more, or $210. Therefore, the sum of $(300 + 40 + 140 + x) = 4(210) = 840$, and $x = \$360$.

7. **30:** Elena's score was within 2 standard deviations of the mean. Since the standard deviation is 15, her score is no more than 30 points from the mean. The lowest possible score she could have received, then, is $60 - 30$, or 30.

8. **5:** Before the $1,000 commission, Milo's average commission was $250; this is expressed algebraically by the equation $S = 250n$.

After the sale, the sum of Milo's sales increased by $1,000, the number of sales made increased by 1, and his average commission was $400. This is expressed algebraically by the equation:

$$S + 1,000 = 400(n + 1)$$
$$250n + 1,000 = 400(n + 1) \qquad 400 \text{ (new)} - (15) \text{ increase} = 240 \text{ (old)}$$
$$250n + 1,000 = 400n + 400$$
$$150n = 600$$
$$n = 4$$

Before the big sale, Milo had made 4 sales. Including the big sale, Milo has made 5 sales.

9. **210:** Grace wants to raise her average score by 10%. Since 10% of 150 is 15, her target average is 165. Grace's total score is 150×6, which is 900. If, in 8 games, she wants to have an average score of 165, then she will need a total score of 165×8, which is 1,320. This is a difference of $1,320 - 900$, which is 420. Her average score in the next two games must be $420 \div 2$, which equals 210.

10. **60:** The sum of two numbers is twice their average. Therefore:

$$x + y = 100 \qquad\qquad y + z = 160$$

$$x = 100 - y \qquad\qquad z = 160 - y$$

Substitute these expressions for z and x:

$$z - x = (160 - y) - (100 - y) = 160 - y - 100 + y = 160 - 100 = 60$$

Alternatively, pick Smart Numbers for x and y. Let $x = 50$ and $y = 50$ (this is an easy way to make their average equal 50). Since the average of y and z must be 80, $z = 110$. Therefore: $z - x = 110 - 50 = 60$.

11. **3.76:** If the range of the list is 7 and $x > 0$, then x^2 has to be the largest number in the list and $x^2 - 1 = 7$. Therefore, $x^2 = 8$ so $x = 2\sqrt{2}$. The average of the list is thus $\dfrac{1 + 2 + 2\sqrt{2} + 5 + 8}{5} = \dfrac{16 + 2\sqrt{2}}{5}$, which is approximately $3.2 + \dfrac{2.8}{5}$, or 3.76.

12. $\dfrac{20}{49}$**:** Since the list is given in order, you can see that the largest item in Quartile 2 is the eighth item

in the list, which is 10. Furthermore the items in Quartile 4 are 23, 24, 25, and 26, and their average is $\dfrac{23 + 24 + 25 + 26}{4}$ which equals 24.5. (Note that these numbers are an evenly spaced list, so the average equals the median or middle number.)

Thus, the ratio is $\dfrac{10}{24.5} = \dfrac{20}{49}$.

13. $\dfrac{1}{3}$**:** If 2% of the observations are below -10, then -10 must approximately be 2 standard deviations from the mean. Thus the standard deviation is approximately $\dfrac{|-10|}{2} \approx 5$, and thus roughly $\dfrac{2}{3}$ of the observations will fall between -5 and 5. Since normal variables are symmetric around the mean, half of that will be in the 0–5 range, so the correct answer is $\left(\dfrac{1}{2}\right)\left(\dfrac{2}{3}\right) = \dfrac{2}{6}$, which simplifies to $\dfrac{1}{3}$.

14. **(B):** This is a Weighted Average problem. The overall average score can be computed by assigning weights to the average scores of Poets and Bards that reflect the number of people in each subgroup. Because the ratio of Poets to Bards is 3 to 2, and collectively the two groups account for all students, the multiple ratio may be written as $P : B : Total = 3 : 2 : 5$.

This means that Poets constitute 3/5 of the students and Bards the remaining 2/5. Therefore, the overall average score is given by the weighted average formula:

$$\frac{3}{5} \times 60 + \frac{2}{5} \times 80 = 68$$

Alternatively, you may argue as follows: if there were the same number of Poets as there were Bards, the overall average score would be 70. However, there are actually more Poets than Bards, so the overall average score will be closer to 60 than to 80 (i.e., less than 70). Therefore, **Quantity B is greater**.

15. **(B):** Begin with the median. In a set with an odd number of terms, the median will be the middle term when the terms are put in ascending order. It is clear that $x + 1 > x - 4$. Moreover, because $x > 2$, $4x$ must be greater than $x + 1$. Therefore, the median is $x + 1$. Rewrite Quantity A:

Quantity A	**Quantity B**
The median of $x - 4$, $x + 1$, and $4x = \boldsymbol{x + 1}$	The mean of $x - 4$, $x + 1$, and $4x$

In order to compute the mean, add all three terms and divide by 3:

$$\text{mean} = \frac{(x-4)+(x+1)+4x}{3} = \frac{6x-3}{3} = 2x - 1$$

Rewrite Quantity B:

Quantity A	**Quantity B**
The median of $x - 4$, $x + 1$, and $4x = \boldsymbol{x + 1}$	The mean of $x - 4$, $x + 1$, and $4x = \boldsymbol{2x - 1}$

The comparison thus boils down to which is greater, $x + 1$ or $2x - 1$. The answer is not immediately clear. Subtract x from both sides to try and isolate x:

Quantity A	**Quantity B**
$x + 1$	$2x - 1$
$\underline{-x}$	$\underline{-x}$
1	$x - 1$

Now add 1 to both sides to isolate x:

Quantity A	Quantity B
$1 + 1 = 2$	$(x - 1) + 1 = x$

The question stem states that x must be greater than 2, therefore, **Quantity B is greater**.

16. **(C):** The sets in question are $A = \{1, 3, 5, 7, 9\}$ and $B = \{2, 4, 6, 8, 10\}$. Each is a set of evenly spaced integers with an odd number of terms, such that the mean is the middle number. The deviations between the elements of the set and the mean of the set in each case are the same: -4, -2, 0, 2, and 4. Thus, the standard deviations of the sets must also be the same. Therefore, **the two quantities are equal**.

5

Chapter 6

of

Word Problems

Combinatorics

In This Chapter...

Chapter 6

Combinatorics

Many GRE problems are, ultimately, just about counting things. Although counting may seem to be a simple concept, *problems about counting* can be complex. In fact, counting problems have given rise to a whole subfield of mathematics: *combinatorics*, which is essentially "advanced counting." This chapter presents the fundamentals of combinatorics that are essential on the GRE.

In combinatorics, you are often counting the **number of possibilities**, such as: How many different ways you can arrange things? For instance, you might ask the following:

- A restaurant menu features 5 appetizers, 6 entrées, and 3 desserts. If a dinner special consists of 1 appetizer, 1 entrée, and 1 dessert, how many different dinner specials are possible?

- Four people sit down in 4 fixed chairs lined up in a row. How many different seating arrangements are possible?

- If there are 7 people in a room, but only 3 chairs in a row, how many different seating arrangements are possible?

- If a group of 3 people is to be chosen from 7 people in a room, how many different groups are possible?

The Fundamental Counting Principle

Counting problems commonly feature multiple separate choices. Whether such choices are made simultaneously (e.g., choosing types of bread and filling for a sandwich) or sequentially (e.g., choosing among routes between successive towns on a road trip), the rule for counting the number of options is the same.

Fundamental Counting Principle: If you must make a number of *separate* decisions, then MULTIPLY the numbers of ways to make each *individual* decision to find the number of ways to make *all* the decisions.

To grasp this principle intuitively, imagine that you are making a simple sandwich. You will choose ONE type of bread out of 2 types (Rye or Whole wheat) and ONE type of filling out of 3 types (chicken salad, peanut butter, or tuna fish). How many different kinds of sandwich can you make? Well, you can always list all the possibilities:

Rye – Chicken salad	Whole wheat – Chicken salad
Rye – Peanut butter	Whole wheat – Peanut butter
Rye – Tuna fish	Whole wheat – Tuna fish

There are six possible sandwiches overall in this table. Instead of listing all the sandwiches, however, you can simply **multiply** the number of bread choices by the number of filling choices, as dictated by the Fundamental Counting Principle:

$$2 \text{ breads} \times 3 \text{ fillings} = 6 \text{ possible sandwiches}$$

As its name implies, the Fundamental Counting Principle is essential to solving combinatorics problems. It is the basis of many other techniques that appear later in this chapter. You can also use the Fundamental Counting Principle directly. For example:

A restaurant menu features 5 appetizers, 6 entrées, and 3 desserts. If a dinner special consists of 1 appetizer, 1 entrée, and 1 dessert, how many different dinner specials are possible?

This problem features three decisions: an appetizer (which can be chosen in 5 different ways), an entrée (6 ways), and a dessert (3 ways). Since the choices are separate, the total number of dinner specials is the product of $5 \times 6 \times 3$, which is 90.

In theory, you could *list* all 90 dinner specials. In practice, that is the last thing you would ever want to do! It would take far too long, and it is likely that you would make a mistake. Multiplying is *much* easier—and more accurate.

Check Your Skills

1. How many ways are there of getting from Alphaville to Gammerburg via Betancourt, if there are 3 roads between Alphaville and Betancourt and 4 roads between Betancourt and Gammerburg?

2. Kyle can choose between blue, black, and brown pants; white, yellow or pink shirts; and whether or not he wears a tie to go with his shirt. How many days can Kyle go without wearing the same combination twice?

Answers can be found on page 119.

Simple Factorials

You are often asked to count the possible arrangements of a set of distinct objects (e.g., "Four people sit down in 4 fixed chairs lined up in a row. How many different seating arrangements are possible?") To count these arrangements, use *factorials*:

The number of ways of putting *n* distinct objects in order, if there are no restrictions, is *n*! (*n* factorial).

The term "*n* factorial" (*n*!) refers to the product of all the positive integers from 1 through *n*, inclusive: $n! = (n)(n-1)(n-2) \ldots (3)(2)(1)$. You should *memorize* the factorials through 6!:

$$1! = 1 \qquad\qquad 4! = 4 \times 3 \times 2 \times 1 = 24$$
$$2! = 2 \times 1 = 2 \qquad\qquad 5! = 5 \times 4 \times 3 \times 2 \times 1 = 120$$
$$3! = 3 \times 2 \times 1 = 6 \qquad\qquad 6! = 6 \times 5 \times 4 \times 3 \times 2 \times 1 = 720$$

Thus, *n*! counts the rearrangements of *n* distinct objects as a special (but very common) application of the Slot Method. For example, consider the case of $n = 4$, with 4 people and 4 fixed chairs. Let each slot represent a chair. Place any one of the 4 people in the first chair. You now have only 3 choices for the person in the second chair. Next, you have 2 choices for the third chair. Finally, you must put the last person in the last chair: you only have 1 choice. Now multiply together all those separate choices:

$$\text{Arrangements of 4 people in 4 fixed chairs: } \underline{4} \times \underline{3} \times \underline{2} \times \underline{1} = 4! = 24$$

Incidentally, you can certainly use the Slot Method the first few times to ensure that you grasp this formula, but then you should graduate to using the formula directly. Try another example:

> In staging a house, a real estate agent must place 6 different books on a bookshelf. In how many different orders can she arrange the books?

Using the Fundamental Counting Principle, you have 6 choices for the book that goes first, 5 choices for the book that goes next, and so forth. Ultimately, you have this total:

$$6! = \underline{6} \times \underline{5} \times \underline{4} \times \underline{3} \times \underline{2} \times \underline{1} = 720 \text{ different orders}$$

Check Your Skills

3. In how many different ways can the 5 Olympic rings be colored Black, Red, Green, Yellow, and Blue, without changing the arrangement of the rings themselves?

The answer can be found on page 119.

6

Anagrams

An *anagram* is a rearrangement of the letters in a word or phrase. (Puzzle enthusiasts require the rearrangement itself to be a meaningful word or phrase, but this section will also include rearrangements that are total nonsense.) For instance, the word DEDUCTIONS is an anagram of DISCOUNTED, and so is the gibberish "word" CDDEINOSTU.

Now that you know about factorials, you can easily count the anagrams of a simple word with n distinct letters: simply compute $n!$ (n factorial). For example:

> How many different anagrams (meaningful or nonsense) are possible for the word GRE?

Since there are 3 distinct letters in the word GRE, there are 3!, which equals $3 \times 2 \times 1$, so there are 6 anagrams of the word.

Check Your Skills

4. In how many different ways can the letters of the word DEPOSIT be arranged (meaningful or nonsense)?

The answer can be found on page 119.

Combinatorics with Repetition: Anagram Grids

Anagrams themselves are unlikely to appear on the GRE. However, many combinatorics problems are exact analogues of anagram problems and can therefore be solved with the same methods developed for the preceding problem. *Most problems involving rearranging objects can be solved by anagramming.* For example:

> If 7 people board an airport shuttle with only 3 available seats, how many different seating arrangements are possible? (Assume that 3 of the 7 will actually take the seats.)

Three of the people will take the seats (designated 1, 2, and 3), and the other four will be left standing (designated "S"). The problem is therefore equivalent to finding anagrams of the "word" 123SSSS, where the 4 S's are equivalent and indistinguishable. Therefore, you have to "uncount" *different arrangements* of them when calculating the number of possible arrangements. You can construct an **Anagram Grid** to help you make the connection:

Person	A	B	C	D	E	F	G
Seat	1	2	3	S	S	S	S

The top row corresponds to the 7 unique people. The bottom row corresponds to the "seating labels" that you put on those people. Note that some of these labels are repeated (the 4 S's). In general, you should set up an Anagram Grid to put the unique items or people on top. Only the bottom row should contain any repeated labels.

In this grid, you are free to rearrange the elements in the bottom row (the 3 seat numbers and the 4 S's), making "anagrams" that represent all the possible seating arrangements. The number of arrangements is therefore:

$$\frac{7!}{4!} = \frac{7 \times 6 \times 5 \times 4 \times 3 \times 2 \times 1}{4 \times 3 \times 2 \times 1} = 7 \times 6 \times 5 = 210$$

Again, divide by 4!, because the 4! ways of arranging the S's are *irrelevant*.

Now consider this problem:

> If 3 of 7 standby passengers are selected for a flight, how many different combinations of standby passengers can be selected?

At first, this problem may seem identical to the previous one, because it also involves selecting three elements out of a set of seven. However, there is a crucial difference. This time, the three "chosen ones" are *also* indistinguishable, whereas in the earlier problem, the three seats on the shuttle were considered different. As a result, you designate all three flying passengers as *F*'s. The four non-flying passengers are still designated as *N*'s. The problem is then equivalent to finding anagrams of the "word" *FFFNNNN*. Again, you can use an Anagram Grid:

Person	A	B	C	D	E	F	G
Seat	F	F	F	N	N	N	N

To calculate the number of possibilities, follow the same rule—factorial of the total, divided by the factorials of the repeated letters on the bottom. But notice that this grid is different from the previous one, in which you had *123NNNNN* in the bottom row. Here, you divide by *two* factorials, 3! for the *F*'s and 4! for the *N*'s, yielding a much smaller number:

$$\frac{7!}{3! \times 4!} = \frac{7 \times 6 \times 5 \times 4 \times 3 \times 2 \times 1}{(3 \times 2 \times 1) \times (4 \times 3 \times 2 \times 1)} = 7 \times 5 = 35$$

Check Your Skills

5. Peggy will choose 5 of her 8 friends to join her for intramural volleyball. In how many ways can she do so?

The answer can be found on page 119.

Multiple Arrangements

So far, our discussion of combinatorics has revolved around two major topics: 1) the Fundamental Counting Principle and its implications for successive choices, and 2) the anagram approach. The GRE will often *combine* these two ideas on more difficult combinatorics problems, requiring you to choose successive or **multiple arrangements**.

If a GRE problem requires you to choose two or more sets of items from separate pools, count the arrangements *separately*—perhaps using a different anagram grid each time. Then multiply the numbers of possibilities for each step.

Distinguish these problems—which require choices from *separate pools*—from complex problems that are still single arrangements (all items chosen from the *same pool*). For instance, a problem requiring the choice of 1 treasurer, 1 secretary, and 3 more representatives from *one* class of 20 students may seem like two or more separate problems, but it is just one: an anagram of 1 T, 1 S, 3 R's, and 15 N's in one 20-letter "word." Try another example:

> The I Eta Pi fraternity must choose a delegation of 3 senior members and 2 junior members for an annual interfraternity conference. If I Eta Pi has 12 senior members and 11 junior members, how many different delegations are possible?

This problem involves two genuinely different arrangements: 3 seniors chosen from a pool of 12 seniors, and 2 juniors chosen from a *separate* pool of 11 juniors. These arrangements should be calculated separately.

Because the three spots in the delegation are not distinguishable, choosing the seniors is equivalent to choosing an anagram of 3 Y's and 9 N's, which can be accomplished in $\dfrac{12!}{9! \times 3!} = 220$ different ways. Similarly, choosing the juniors is equivalent to choosing an anagram of 2 Y's and 9 N's, which can be done in $\dfrac{11!}{9! \times 2!} = 55$ different ways.

Since the choices are successive and independent, to get the answer, simply multiply the numbers: $220 \times 55 = 12{,}100$ different delegations are possible.

Check Your Skills

6. Three men (out of 7) and 3 women (out of 6) will be chosen to serve on a committee. In how many ways can the committee be formed?

The answer can be found on page 119.

Check Your Skills Answer Key

1. **12:** Multiply the number of choices for each leg of the trip: $3 \times 4 = 12$.

2. **18:** Kyle has 3 choices of pants, 3 choices of shirts, and 2 choices involving a tie (yes or no). Therefore, his total number of choices is $3 \times 3 \times 2$, which is 18.

3. **120:** This question is asking for the number of ways to order 5 colored rings with no restrictions. Thus:

$$5! = \underline{5} \times \underline{4} \times \underline{3} \times \underline{2} \times \underline{1} = 120$$

4. **5,040:** A 7-letter word with all distinct letters has $7! = 7 \times 6 \times 5 \times 4 \times 3 \times 2 \times 1 = 5{,}040$ anagrams.

5. **56:** Produce an Anagram Grid using 1 through 8 for the friends, Y for Yes (i.e., joining Peggy), and N for No (not joining Peggy):

Friend	1	2	3	4	5	6	7	8
Status	Y	Y	Y	Y	Y	N	N	N

Anagram the "word" $YYYYYNNN$: $\dfrac{8!}{5!3!} = \dfrac{8 \times 7 \times 6 \times 5 \times 4 \times 3 \times 2 \times 1}{(5 \times 4 \times 3 \times 2 \times 1) \times (3 \times 2 \times 1)} = \dfrac{8 \times 7 \times 6}{3 \times 2 \times 1} = 56$.

6. **700:** For the men, anagram the word $YYYNNNN$: $\dfrac{7!}{3!4!} = \dfrac{7 \times 6 \times 5 \times 4 \times 3 \times 2 \times 1}{(3 \times 2 \times 1)(4 \times 3 \times 2 \times 1)} = \dfrac{7 \times 6 \times 5}{3 \times 2 \times 1} = 35$.

For the women, anagram the word $YYYNNN$: $\dfrac{6!}{3!3!} = \dfrac{6 \times 5 \times 4 \times 3 \times 2 \times 1}{(3 \times 2 \times 1)(3 \times 2 \times 1)} = \dfrac{6 \times 5 \times 4}{3 \times 2 \times 1} = 20$.

Multiply the choices to get the total: $35 \times 20 = 700$ ways. (This is considerably fewer than the number of ways to choose 6 out of 13 people without regard to gender.)

6

Problem Set

Solve the following problems using the strategies you have learned in this section.

1. In how many different ways can the letters in the word LEVEL be arranged?

2. Alina and Adam are making boxes of truffles to give out as wedding favors. They have an unlimited supply of 5 different types of truffles. If each box holds 2 truffles of different types, how many different boxes can they make?

3. A men's basketball league assigns every player a two-digit number for the back of his jersey. If the league uses only the digits 1–5, what is the maximum number of players that can join the league such that no player has a number with a repeated digit (e.g., 22), and no two players have the same number?

4. A pod of 6 dolphins always swims single file, with 3 females at the front and 3 males in the rear. In how many different arrangements can the dolphins swim?

5. A delegation from Gotham City goes to Metropolis to discuss a limited Batman–Superman partnership. If the mayor of Metropolis chooses 3 members of the 7-person delegation to meet with Superman, how many different 3-person combinations can he choose?

6. Mario's Pizza has 2 choices of crust: deep dish crust or thin crust. The restaurant also has a choice of 5 toppings: tomatoes, sausage, peppers, onions, and pepperoni. Finally, Mario's offers every pizza in extra cheese as well as regular. If Linda's volleyball team decides to order a pizza with 4 unique toppings, how many different choices do the teammates have at Mario's Pizza?

7. Country X has a four-digit postal code assigned to each town, such that the first digit is non-zero, and none of the digits is repeated.

Quantity A	**Quantity B**
The number of possible postal codes in Country X	4,500

8. Eight athletes compete in a race in which a gold, a silver and a bronze medal will be awarded to the top three finishers, in that order.

Quantity A	Quantity B
The number of ways in which the medals can be awarded	$8 \times 3!$

9. Lothar has 6 stamps from Utopia and 4 stamps from Cornucopia in his collection. He will give two stamps of each type to his friend Peggy Sue.

Quantity A	Quantity B
The number of ways Lothar can give 4 stamps (two of each type) to Peggy Sue	100

6

Solutions

1. **30:** There are two repeated *E*'s and two repeated *L*'s in the word *LEVEL*. To find the anagrams for this word, set up a fraction in which the numerator is the factorial of the number of letters and the denominator is the factorial of the number of each repeated letter:

$$\frac{5!}{2!2!} = \frac{5 \times 4 \times 3 \times 2 \times 1}{2 \times 1 \times 2 \times 1} = 30$$

Alternatively, you can solve this problem using the Slot Method, as long as you correct for over-counting (since you have some indistinguishable elements). There are 5 choices for the first letter, 4 for the second, and so on, making the product $5 \times 4 \times 3 \times 2 \times 1$, which is 120. However, there are two sets of 2 indistinguishable elements each, so you must divide by 2! to account for each of these. Thus, the total number of combinations is $\frac{5 \times 4 \times 3 \times 2 \times 1}{2! \times 2!} = 30$.

2. **10:** In every combination, 2 types of truffles will be in the box, and 3 types of truffles will not. Therefore, this problem is a question about the number of anagrams that can be made from the "word" *YYNNN*:

$$\frac{5!}{2!3!} = \frac{5 \times 4 \times 3 \times 2 \times 1}{(3 \times 2 \times 1) \times (2 \times 1)} = 5 \times 2 = 10$$

A	B	C	D	E
Y	Y	N	N	N

This problem can also be solved with the formula for combinations, since it is a combination of 2 items chosen from a set of 5 (in which order does not matter). Therefore, there are $\frac{5!}{2! \times 3!} = 10$ possible combinations.

3. **20:** In this problem, the order of the numbers matters. Each number can be either the tens digit, the units digit, or not a digit in the number. Therefore, this problem is a question about the number of anagrams that can be made from the "word" *TUNNN*:

$$\frac{5!}{3!} = \frac{5 \times 4 \times 3 \times 2 \times 1}{3 \times 2 \times 1} = 5 \times 4 = 20$$

1	2	3	4	5
T	U	N	N	N

You can also use the Slot Method. The slots correspond to the positions of the digits (tens and units). You have 5 choices for the tens digit and then only 4 choices for the units digit (since you cannot use the same digit again), resulting in $5 \times 4 = 20$ possibilities. This method works well for problems in which order matters.

Finally, you can just list out the jersey numbers, since the number of possibilities is relatively small. Even if you stop partway through, this can be a good way to start, so that you get a sense of the problem:

12, 13, 14, 15, 21, 23, 24, 25, 31, 32, 34, 35, 41, 42, 43, 45, 51, 52, 53, 54 = 5 groups of 4 = 20

4. 36: There are 3! ways in which the 3 females can swim. There are 3! ways in which the 3 males can swim. Therefore, there are 3! × 3! ways in which the entire pod can swim:

$$3! \times 3! = 3 \times 2 \times 1 \times 3 \times 2 \times 1 = 6 \times 6 = 36$$

This is a multiple arrangements problem, in which you have two separate pools (females and males).

5. 35: Model this problem with anagrams for the "word" *YYYNNNN*, in which 3 people are in the delegation and 4 are not:

$$\frac{7!}{3!4!} = \frac{7 \times 6 \times 5}{3 \times 2 \times 1} = 35 \qquad \text{Note that you must divide by both 3! and 4! in this problem.}$$

Alternatively, you can use the anagram method, because this problem requires the number of possible combinations of 3 delegates taken from a total of 7. (Note that order does not matter.) Therefore, the number of possible combinations is $\frac{7!}{3! \times 4!} = 35$.

A	B	C	D	E	F	G
Y	Y	Y	N	N	N	N

6. 20: Consider the toppings first. Model the toppings with the "word" *YYYYN*, in which 4 of the toppings are on the pizza and 1 is not. The number of anagrams for this "word" is:

$$\frac{5!}{4!} = 5$$

A	B	C	D	E
Y	Y	Y	Y	N

If each of these pizzas can also be offered in 2 choices of crust, there are 5 × 2 = 10 pizzas. The same logic applies for extra cheese and regular: 10 × 2 = 20.

Alternatively, use the combinations formula to count the combinations of toppings: $\frac{5!}{4! \times 1!} = 5$. Or use an intuitive approach: choosing 4 toppings out of 5 is equivalent to choosing the 1 topping that will not be on the pizza. There are clearly 5 ways to do that.

7. (A): You can use the Slot Method to solve this problem. The first slot can be filled by any one of the digits from 1 through 9, since 0 is disallowed. The second digit has no restriction involving 0; however, the digit that was used in the first slot may not be reused. Thus, the second slot also has 9 possibilities. The third and fourth slots may not use previously used digits, so they may be filled with 8 and 7 different digits, respectively. The total number of possible postal codes is therefore:

$$9 \times 9 \times 8 \times 7 = 4{,}536 \quad$$

Quantity A	Quantity B
The number of possible postal codes in Country X = **4,536**	4,500

Therefore, **Quantity A is greater**.

8. **(A):** The Anagram Grid is a good method for solving this problem. Use the numbers 1 through 8 to uniquely designate each athlete. In the second row, *G, S,* and *B* designate the 3 medals, while the athletes who get no medal can each be associated with an *N*:

Athlete	1	2	3	4	5	6	7	8
Medal	*G*	*S*	*B*	*N*	*N*	*N*	*N*	*N*

The number of ways the medals can be awarded is the number of ways the "word" *GSBNNNNN* can be anagrammed. Because 5 of the letters are repeated, the answer is given by:

$$\frac{8!}{5!} = \frac{8 \times 7 \times 6 \times 5 \times 4 \times 3 \times 2 \times 1}{5 \times 4 \times 3 \times 2 \times 1} = 8 \times 7 \times 6$$

Compare this number to $8 \times 3!$:

$$8 \times 3! = 8 \times 3 \times 2 \times 1 = 8 \times 6$$

Rewrite the quantities:

Quantity A	Quantity B
The number of ways in which the medals can be awarded = **8 × 7 × 6**	$8 \times 3! = \mathbf{8 \times 6}$

Therefore, **Quantity A is greater**.

9. **(B):** This exercise can be regarded as two successive "pick a group" problems. First, Lothar picks 2 out of 6 Utopian stamps, and then 2 out of 4 Cornucopian stamps. Each selection may be computed by using the Anagram Word formula to compute the number of groups of size 2 of each type of stamp. To get the total number of ways, the two numbers thus obtained must then be multiplied to give the final result:

$$\text{Total number of ways } = \left(\frac{6!}{2!4!}\right) \times \left(\frac{4!}{2!2!}\right) = \left(\frac{6 \times 5}{2 \times 1}\right) \times \left(\frac{4 \times 3}{2 \times 1}\right) = 15 \times 6 = 90$$

Quantity A	**Quantity B**
The number of ways Lothar can give four stamps (two of each type) to Peggy Sue = **90**	100

Therefore, **Quantity B is greater**.

Chapter 7
of

Word Problems

Probability

In This Chapter...

Chapter 7
Probability

Probability is a quantity that expresses the chance, or likelihood, of an event. In other words, it measures how often an event will occur in a long series of repeated trials.

For events with countable outcomes, probability is defined by the following fraction:

$$\textbf{Probability} = \frac{\textbf{Number of } \textit{desired} \textbf{ or } \textit{successful} \textbf{ outcomes}}{\textbf{Total number of } \textit{possible} \textbf{ outcomes}}$$

This fraction assumes all *outcomes are equally likely.* If not, the math can be more complicated (more on this later).

As a simple illustration, rolling a die (singular for dice) has six possible outcomes: 1, 2, 3, 4, 5, and 6. The probability of rolling a "5" is 1/6, because the "5" corresponds to only one of those outcomes. The probability of rolling a prime number, though, is 3/6, which simplifies to 1/2, because in that case, three of the outcomes—2, 3, and 5—are considered successes.

Again, all the outcomes must be equally likely. For instance, you could say that the lottery has only two "outcomes"—win or lose—but that does not mean the probability of winning the lottery is 1/2. If you want to calculate the correct probability of winning the lottery, you must find *all of the possible* equally likely outcomes. In other words, you have to count up all the specific combinations of differently numbered balls in the lottery to determine the correct probability of winning the lottery.

In some problems, you will have to think carefully about how to break a situation down into equally likely outcomes. Consider the following problem:

> If a fair coin is tossed three times, what is the probability that it will turn up heads exactly twice?

You may be tempted to say that there are four possibilities—no heads, 1 head, 2 heads, and 3 heads—and that the probability of 2 heads is thus 1/4. You would be wrong, though, because those four

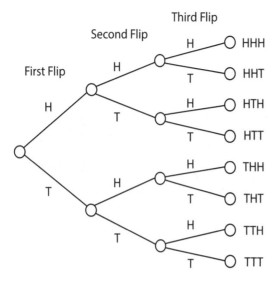

outcomes are not equally likely. You are much more likely to get 1 or 2 heads than to get all heads or all tails. Instead, you have to formulate equally likely outcomes in terms of the outcome of each flip:

HHH HHT HTH THH HTT THT
TTH TTT

If you have trouble formulating this list from scratch, you can use a **counting tree**, which breaks down possible outcomes step by step, with only one decision at each branch of the tree. An example is to the left.

These eight outcomes are equally likely, because the coin is equally likely to come up heads or tails at each flip. Three outcomes on this list (HHT, HTH, THH) have heads exactly twice, so the probability of exactly two heads is 3/8.

This result can also be written:

P(exactly 2 heads) = 3/8.

"1" Is the Greatest Probability

The greatest probability—the *certainty* that an event will occur—is 1. Thus, a probability of 1 means that the event must occur. For example:

The probability that you roll a fair die once, and it lands on a number less than seven, is certain, or 1:

$$\frac{\text{Number of }successful\text{ outcomes}}{\text{Total number of possible outcomes}} = \frac{6}{6} = \mathbf{1}$$

As a percent, this certainty is expressed as 100%.

The lowest probability—the *impossibility* that an event will occur—is 0. Thus, a probability of 0 means that an event will NOT occur. For example, the probability that you roll a fair die once and it lands on the number 9 is impossible—a probability of 0:

$$\frac{\text{Number of }successful\text{ outcomes}}{\text{Total number of possible outcomes}} = \frac{0}{6} = \mathbf{0}$$

As a percent, this impossibility is expressed as 0%.

Thus, probabilities can also be expressed as percents between 0% and 100%, inclusive, or fractions between 0 and 1, inclusive.

More Than One Event: "AND" vs. "OR"

Probability problems that deal with multiple events usually involve two primary operations: multiplication and addition. The key to understanding probability is to understand *when you must multiply* and *when you must add.*

Assume that X and Y are *independent* events. Two events are said to be *independent* if the likelihood of one occurring does not depend on the likelihood of the other occurring. **To determine the probability that event X AND event Y will both occur, MULTIPLY the two probabilities together.** Note that the events must be independent for this to work! For example:

> What is the probability that a fair coin flipped twice will land on heads both times?

This is an "AND" problem, because it is asking for the probability that the coin will land on heads on the first flip AND on the second flip. The probability that the coin will land on heads on the first flip is 1/2. The probability that the coin will land on heads on the second flip is 1/2. These events *are* independent of each other.

Therefore, to determine the probability that the coin will land on heads on both flips, multiply the probabilities: $\frac{1}{2} \times \frac{1}{2} = \frac{1}{4}$.

Note that the probability of having BOTH flips come up heads (1/4) is less than the probability of having just one flip come up heads (1/2). This should make intuitive sense. If you define success in a more constrained way (e.g., "to win, BOTH this AND that have to happen"), then the probability of success will be lower. The operation of multiplication should also make sense. Typical probabilities are fractions between 0 and 1. When you multiply together two such fractions, you get a *smaller* result, which means a lower probability.

Now assume that X and Y are *mutually exclusive* events (meaning that the two events cannot both occur). **To determine the probability that event X OR event Y will occur, ADD the two probabilities together.** For example:

> What is the probability that a fair die rolled once will land on *either* 4 or 5?

This is an "OR" problem, because it is asking for the probability that the die will land on either 4 **OR** 5. The probability that the die will land on 4 is 1/6. The probability that the die will land on 5 is 1/6. The two outcomes are mutually exclusive: the die cannot land on BOTH 4 and 5 at the same time.

Therefore, to find the probability that the die will land on either 4 or 5, add the probabilities: $\frac{1}{6} + \frac{1}{6} = \frac{2}{6} = \frac{1}{3}$.

Note that the probability of having the die come up either 4 or 5 (1/3) is greater than the probability of a 4 by itself (1/6) or of a 5 by itself (1/6). This should make intuitive sense. If you define success in a less constrained way (e.g., "I can win EITHER this way OR that way"), then the probability of success will be higher. The operation of addition should also make sense. Typical probabilities are fractions between 0 and 1. When you add together two such fractions, you get a *larger* result, which means a higher probability.

That said, the vast majority of probability questions on the GRE are of the "AND" variety. Thus, when in doubt; most GRE probability problems just want you to multiply two or three fractions together.

Check Your Skills

1. If a die is rolled twice, what is the probability that it will land on an even number both times?

2. Eight runners in a race are equally likely to win the race. What is the probability that the race will be won by the runner in lane 1 OR the runner in lane 8?

Answers can be found on page 137.

Advanced note: For adding "OR" probabillities, up until now it has been assumed that the events are *mutually exclusive* (meaning that both events cannot occur). What happens if the events are *not* mutually exclusive?

If that is the case, and you simply add the probabilities, you will be double-counting the instances when *both* events occur. Thus, you must *subtract out* the probability that both events occur.

If events X and Y are not mutually exclusive, then $P(X \text{ OR } Y) = P(X) + P(Y) - P(X \text{ AND } Y)$. For example:

> Suppose a box contains 20 balls. Ten balls are white and marked with the integers 1–10. The other 10 balls are red and marked with the integers 11–20. If one ball is selected, what is the probability that the ball will be white OR will be marked with an even number?

Since half the balls are white and half are marked with an even number $P(\text{white}) + P(\text{even})$ would give you $\frac{1}{2} + \frac{1}{2}$, which equals 1. **This is incorrect!** You must subtract out the probability that the ball is both white AND marked with an even number. There are 5 such balls out of 20. Thus, the correct answer is: $P(\text{white or even}) = P(\text{white}) + P(\text{even}) - P(\text{white AND even}) = \frac{1}{2} + \frac{1}{2} - \frac{5}{20} = 1 - \frac{1}{4} = \frac{3}{4}$.

Check Your Skills

3. A fair die is rolled and a fair coin is flipped. What is the probability that either the die will come up 2 or 3, OR the coin will land heads up?

The answer can be found on page 137.

The "1 − x" Probability Trick

As shown in the previous section, you can solve "OR" problems (explicit or disguised) by combining the probabilities of individual events. If there are many individual events, though, such calculation may be tedious and time-consuming. The good news is that you may not have to perform these calculations. In certain types of "OR" problems, the probability of the desired event not happening may be much easier to calculate.

For example, in the previous section, you could have calculated the probability of getting at least one head on two flips by considering how you would NOT get at least one head. However, it would not be too much work to compute the probability directly, using the slightly more complicated "OR" formula.

But say that a salesperson makes five sales calls, and you want to find the likelihood that he or she makes *at least* one sale. If you try to calculate this probability directly, you will have to confront five separate possibilities that constitute "success": exactly 1 sale, exactly 2 sales, exactly 3 sales, exactly 4 sales, or exactly 5 sales. It would seem that you would have no choice but to calculate each of those probabilities separately and then add them together. This will be far too much work, especially under timed conditions.

However, consider the probability of *failure*—that is, the salesperson *does not* make at least one sale. Now you have only one possibility to consider: 0 sales. You can now calculate the probability in which you are interested, because for *any* event, the following relationship is true:

Probability of SUCCESS + Probability of FAILURE = 1
(the event happens)   (it does *not* happen)

*If, on a GRE problem, "success" contains **multiple possibilities**—especially if the wording contains phrases such as **"at least"** and **"at most"**—then consider finding the probability that success **does not happen**. If you can find this "failure" probability more easily (call it x), then the probability you really want to find will be **1 − x**. For example:*

> What is the probability that, on three rolls of a single fair die, AT LEAST ONE of the rolls will be a 6?

You could list all the possible outcomes of three rolls of a die (1–1–1, 1–1–2, 1–1–3, etc.), and then determine how many of them have at least one 6, but this would be very time-consuming. Instead, it is easier to think of this problem in reverse before solving:

> Failure: What is the probability that NONE of the rolls will yield a 6?

On each roll, there is a $\dfrac{5}{6}$ probability that the die will NOT yield a 6. Thus, the probability that on all three rolls the die will *not* yield a 6 is: $\dfrac{5}{6} \times \dfrac{5}{6} \times \dfrac{5}{6} = \dfrac{125}{216}$.

Now, success was originally defined as rolling at least one 6. Since you have found the probability of failure, you can answer the original question by subtracting this probability from 1:

$$1 - \frac{125}{216} = \frac{91}{216}$$ is the probability that at least one six will be rolled.

Check Your Skills

4. If a die is rolled twice, what is the probability that it will land on an even number at least once?

The answer can be found on page 137.

The Domino Effect

Sometimes the outcome of the first event will affect the probability of a subsequent event. For example:

> In a box with 10 blocks, 3 of which are red, what is the probability of picking out a red block on each of your first two tries? Assume that you do NOT replace the first block after you have picked it.

Since this is an "AND" problem, you must find the probability of both events and multiply them together. Consider how easy it is to make the following mistake:

You compute the probability of picking a red block on your first pick as $\frac{3}{10}$.

You compute the probability of picking a red block on your second pick as $\frac{3}{10}$.

So you compute the probability of picking a red block on both picks as $\frac{3}{10} \times \frac{3}{10} = \frac{9}{100}$.

This solution is WRONG, because it does not take into account that the first event affects the second event; this means that the two events are NOT *independent*, so you cannot simply multiply their probabilities to calculate their combined probability. If a red block is chosen on the first pick, then the number of blocks now in the box has decreased from **10 to 9**. Additionally, the number of red blocks now in the box has decreased from **3 to 2**. Therefore, the probability of choosing a red block on the second pick is different from the probability of choosing a red block on the first pick.

The CORRECT solution to this problem is as follows:

The probability of picking a red block on your first pick is $\frac{3}{10}$.

The probability of picking a red block on your second pick is $\frac{2}{9}$.

Therefore, the probability of picking a red block on both picks is $\frac{3}{10} \times \frac{2}{9} = \frac{6}{90} = \frac{1}{15}$.

Do not forget to analyze events by considering whether one event affects subsequent events. The first roll of a die or flip of a coin has no effect on any subsequent rolls or flips. However, the first pick of an object out of a box *does* affect subsequent picks if you do not replace that object. This scenario is called "no replacement" or "without replacement."

If you *are* supposed to replace the object, the problem should clearly tell you so. In this scenario (called "with replacement"), the first pick does not affect the second pick.

Check Your Skills

5. A drawer contains 7 white shirts and 3 red shirts. What is the probability of picking a white shirt, followed by a red shirt if the first shirt is not put back in?

The answer can be found on page 137.

7

Check Your Skills Answer Key

1. **1/4:** For each throw, the probability of an even number is 3/6, which simplifies to 1/2. Multiply the individual probabilities because the two outcomes are independent: $P = 1/2 \times 1/2 = 1/4$.

2. **1/4:** $P(1) = 1/8$, $P(8) = 1/8$, $P(1 \text{ or } 8) = 1/8 + 1/8 = 2/8 = 1/4$.

3. **2/3:** Rolling a 2 or 3 on the die and flipping a heads on the coin are not mutually exclusive (that is, it is possible for both events to happen). Thus, P(one event OR the other event) = P(one event) + P(the other event) − P(both events). In this scenario, P(2 or 3 on the die) = 1/6 + 1/6 = 2/6. P(heads on the coin) = 1/2 = 3/6. P(both) = 2/6 × 1/2 = 1/6 because the die roll and coin flip are independent events. Therefore, P(2 or 3 OR heads) = 2/6 + 3/6 − 1/6 = 4/6 = 2/3.

4. **3/4:** If the die does not land on an even number at least once, then it must have landed on an odd number both times. For each throw, the probability of an odd number is 3/6 = 1/2. Multiply the individual probabilities to get the probability of two odd numbers in a row: $x = 1/2 \times 1/2 = 1/4$. Then the probability of at least one even number is $1 - x = 1 - 1/4$, which is 3/4.

5. **7/30:** There are 10 shirts total:

    Probability of picking a white shirt first: 7/10.

    Probability of picking a red shirt next (out of 9 remaining): 3/9 = 1/3.

    Probability of picking white first, then red: 7/10 × 3/9 = 21/90 = 7/30.

7

Problem Set

Solve the following problems. Express probabilities as fractions or percentages unless otherwise instructed.

1. What is the probability that the sum of two dice rolls will yield a 4 OR 6?

2. What is the probability that the sum of two dice rolls will yield anything but an 8?

3. What is the probability that the sum of two dice rolls will yield a 7, and then when both are thrown again, their sum will again yield a 7?

4. What is the probability that the sum of two dice rolls will yield a 5, and then when both are thrown again, their sum will yield a 9?

5. At a certain pizzeria, 1/6 of the pizzas sold in a week were cheese, and 1/5 of the OTHER pizzas sold were pepperoni. If Brandon bought a randomly chosen pizza from the pizzeria that week, what is the probability that he ordered a pepperoni?

6. John invites 12 friends to a dinner party, half of whom are men. Exactly one man and one woman are bringing desserts. If one person from this group is selected at random, what is the probability that it is a man who is not bringing a dessert OR that it is a woman?

7. A fair coin is flipped 5 times.

Quantity A	Quantity B
The probability of getting more heads than tails	$\frac{1}{2}$

7

8. A jar contains 3 red and 2 white marbles. Two marbles are picked without replacement.

Quantity A	**Quantity B**
The probability of picking two red marbles	The probability of picking exactly one red and one white marble

9. A die is rolled *n* times, where *n* is at least 3.

Quantity A	**Quantity B**
The probability that at least one of the throws yields a 6	$\dfrac{1}{2}$

Solutions

1. **2/9:** There are 36 ways in which 2 dice can be thrown ($6 \times 6 = 36$). The combinations that yield sums of 4 and 6 are $1 + 3, 2 + 2, 3 + 1, 1 + 5, 2 + 4, 3 + 3, 4 + 2$, and $5 + 1$, for a total of 8 different combinations. Therefore, the probability is 8/36, which simplifies to 2/9.

2. **31/36:** Solve this problem by calculating the probability that the sum WILL yield a sum of 8, and then subtract the result from 1. There are 5 combinations of 2 dice that yield a sum of 8: $2 + 6, 3 + 5,$ $4 + 4, 5 + 3$, and $6 + 2$. (Note that $7 + 1$ is not a valid combination, as there is no 7 on a standard die.) Therefore, the probability that the sum will be 8 is 5/36, and the probability that the sum will NOT be 8 is $1 - 5/36$, which equals 31/36.

3. **1/36:** There are 36 ways in which 2 dice can be thrown ($6 \times 6 = 36$). The combinations that yield a sum of 7 are $1 + 6, 2 + 5, 3 + 4, 4 + 3, 5 + 2$, and $6 + 1$, for a total of 6 different combinations. Therefore, the probability of rolling a 7 is 6/36, which simplifies to 1/6. To find the probability that this will happen twice in a row, multiply 1/6 by 1/6 to get 1/36.

4. **1/81:** First, find the individual probability of each event. The probability of rolling a 5 is 4/36, or 1/9, since there are 4 ways to roll a sum of 5 ($1 + 4, 2 + 3, 3 + 2$, and $4 + 1$). The probability of rolling a 9 is also 4/36, or 1/9, since there are 4 ways to roll a sum of 9 ($3 + 6, 4 + 5, 5 + 4$, and $6 + 3$). To find the probability that both events will happen in succession, multiply: $1/9 \times 1/9 = 1/81$.

5. **1/6:** If 1/6 of the pizzas were cheese, 5/6 of the pizzas were not. Because 1/5 of these 5/6 were pepperoni, multiply to find the total portion: $1/5 \times 5/6 = 5/30 = 1/6$. If 1/6 of the pizzas were pepperoni, there is a 1/6 chance that Brandon bought a pepperoni pizza.

6. $\dfrac{11}{12}$**:** Six women are invited and 5 men *who are not bringing a dessert* are invited. Thus, $6 + 5$, which is 11, out of 12 would fit the description.

7. **(C):** Because heads and tails are equally likely, it follows that the probability of getting more heads than tails should be exactly the same as the probability of getting more tails than heads. The only remaining option is that you might get equally many heads and tails. However, because the total number of coin flips is an odd number, the latter is impossible. Therefore, the probability of getting more heads than tails must be exactly 1/2. (It is, of course, also possible to compute this probability directly by considering the cases of getting 5, 4, or 3 heads separately. However, this approach would be very time-consuming.)

Another way of thinking about it is that, for every set of flips that has more heads than tails, there is a corresponding set of flips, in which every flip gets the opposite result, that has more tails. For instance, the sequence of throws *HHHHH* is balanced by the sequence *TTTTT*. The sequence *HHHHT* is balanced by the sequence *TTTTH*.

Therefore, **the two quantities are equal**.

8. **(B):** First, compute the probability of picking 2 red marbles. This is given by:

$$P(RR) = \frac{3}{5} \times \frac{2}{4} = \frac{3}{10}$$

Next, consider the probability of picking a red marble followed by a white marble:

$$P(RW) = \frac{3}{5} \times \frac{2}{4} = \frac{3}{10}$$

However, this is not the only way to pick 1 red AND 1 white marble; you could have picked the white one first, followed by the red one:

$$P(WR) = \frac{2}{5} \times \frac{3}{4} = \frac{3}{10}$$

This event is mutually exclusive from picking a red marble followed by a white marble. Thus, the total probability of picking 1 red AND 1 white marble is the sum of the probabilities of *RW* and *WR*, yielding an answer of:

$$P(RW \text{ OR } WR) = \frac{3}{10} + \frac{3}{10} = 2 \times \left(\frac{3}{10}\right) = \frac{6}{10} = \frac{3}{5}$$

Quantity A	**Quantity B**
The probability of picking two red marbles = **3/10**	The probability of picking one red and one white marble = **3/5**

Therefore, **Quantity B is greater**.

9. **(D):** The easiest way to compute the probability in question is through the "$1 - x$" shortcut. To do so, imagine the opposite of the event of interest, namely, that *none* of the n throws yields a 6. The probability of a single throw not yielding a 6 is 5/6, and because each throw is independent, the cumulative probability of none of the n throws yielding a 6 is found by multiplication:

$$P(\text{No 6 in } n \text{ throws}) = \left(\frac{5}{6}\right)^n$$

Powers of fractions less than one get smaller as the exponent increases. Thus, this probability will become very small for large values of n, such that the probability of getting at least one 6 (which is $1-\left(\dfrac{5}{6}\right)^{n}$) will come closer and closer to 1. Thus, as n increases, it becomes more and more certain that a 6 will be thrown. The question now is, What is the smallest that the probability of getting at least one six could be? To answer that question, you should set n to its lowest possible value, which is 3. In that case, the probability of never getting a 6 is given by:

$$P(\text{No 6 in three throws}) = \left(\frac{5}{6}\right)^{3} = \frac{125}{216}$$

 Use the calculator to compute the numerator and denominator separately.

However, the probability of getting at least one 6 in three throws is given by:

$$P(\text{At least one 6 in three throws}) = 1 - \frac{125}{216} = \frac{91}{216}$$

This value is less than 1/2. As you saw earlier, however, as n grows, it becomes ever more likely that at least one throw will yield a 6, so that the probability eventually surpasses 1/2. Thus, Quantity A can be less than or greater than 1/2. Thus, **the relationship cannot be determined from the information given**.

7

Chapter 8
of
Word Problems

Minor Problem Types

In This Chapter...

Optimization

Grouping

Overlapping Sets

Chapter 8
Minor Problem Types

The GRE occasionally contains problems that fall into one of three categories:

1. *Optimization*: maximizing or minimizing a quantity by choosing optimal values of related quantities.
2. *Grouping*: putting people or items into different groups to fit some criteria.
3. *Overlapping sets:* people or items that can belong in one of two groups, neither, or both.

You should approach all three of these problem types with the same general outlook, although it is unlikely that you will see more than one of them on the same administration of the GRE. The general approach is to focus on **extreme scenarios**.

You should mind the following three considerations when considering any grouping or optimization problem:

1. Be aware of both ***explicit constraints*** (restrictions actually stated in the text) and ***hidden constraints*** (restrictions implied by the real-world aspects of a problem). For instance, in a problem requiring the separation of 40 people into 6 groups, hidden constraints require the number of people in each group to be a positive whole number.
2. In most cases, you can maximize or minimize quantities (or optimize schedules, etc.) by ***choosing the highest or lowest values*** of the variables that you are allowed to select.
3. For ***overlapping sets***, remember that people/items that fit in both categories lessen the number of people/items in just one category. Thus, all other things being equal, the ***more people/items in "both," the fewer in "just one" and the more in "neither."***

Optimization

In general optimization problems, you are asked to maximize or minimize some quantity, given constraints on other quantities. These quantities are all related through some equation.

Consider the following problem:

> The guests at a football banquet consumed a total of 401 pounds of food. If no individual guest consumed more than 2.5 pounds of food, what is the minimum number of guests that could have attended the banquet?

You can visualize the underlying equation in the following table:

Pounds of food per guest	×	Guests	=	Total pounds of food
At MOST 2.5 *maximize*	×	At LEAST ??? *minimize*	=	EXACTLY 401 *constant*

Notice that finding the *minimum* value of the number of guests involves using the maximum pounds of food per guest, because the two quantities multiply to a constant. This sort of inversion (i.e., maximizing one thing in order to minimize another) is typical.

Begin by considering the extreme case in which each guest eats as much food as possible, or 2.5 pounds apiece. The corresponding number of guests at the banquet works out to 401/2.5 = 160.4 people.

However, you obviously cannot have a fractional number of guests at the banquet. Thus, the answer must be rounded. To determine whether to round up or down, consider the explicit constraint: the amount of food per guest is a *maximum* of 2.5 pounds per guest. Therefore, the *minimum* number of guests is 160.4 (if guests could be fractional), and you must *round up* to make the number of guests an integer: 161.

Note the careful reasoning required! Although the phrase "*minimum* number of guests" may tempt you to round down, you will get an incorrect answer if you do so. In general, as you solve this sort of problem, put the extreme case into the underlying equation, and solve. Then round appropriately.

Check Your Skills

1. If no one in a group of friends has more than $75, what is the smallest number of people who could be in the group if the group purchases a flat-screen TV that costs $1,100?

The answer can be found on page 153.

Grouping

In grouping problems, you make complete groups of items, drawing these items out of a larger pool. The goal is usually to maximize or minimize some quantity, such as the number of complete groups or the number of leftover items that do not fit into complete groups. As such, these problems are often really a special case of optimization problems. One approach is to determine the **limiting factor** on the number of complete groups. That is, if you need different types of items for a complete group, figure out how many groups you can make with each item, ignoring the other types (as if you had unlimited quantities of those other items). Then compare your results. For example:

> Orange Computers is breaking up its conference attendees into groups. Each group must have exactly one person from Division A, two people from Division B, and three people from Division C. There are 20 people from Division A, 30 people from Division B, and 40 people from Division C at the conference. What is the smallest number of people who will NOT be able to be assigned to a group?

The first step is to find out how many groups you can make with the people from each division separately, ignoring the other divisions. There are enough Division A people for 20 groups, but only enough Division B people for 15 groups (= 30 people ÷ 2 people per group). As for Division C, there are only enough people for 13 groups, since 40 people ÷ 3 people per group = 13 groups, plus one person left over. So the limiting factor is Division C: only 13 complete groups can be formed. These 13 groups will take up 13 Division A people (leaving 20 − 13 = 7 left over) and 26 Division B people (leaving 30 − 26 = 4 left over). Together with the 1 Division C person left over, there are 1 + 4 + 7 = 12 people will be left over in total.

For some grouping problems, you may want to think about the **most or least evenly distributed** arrangements of the items. That is, assign items to groups as evenly (or unevenly) as possible to create extreme cases.

Check Your Skills

2. A salad dressing requires oil, vinegar, and water in the ratio 2 : 1 : 3. If Oliver has 1 cup of oil, 1/3 cup of vinegar, and 2 cups of water, what is the maximum number of cups of dressing that he can mix?

The answer can be found on page 153.

8

Overlapping Sets

In overlapping sets, people or items will be categorized by their "membership" or "non-membership" in either of two groups. For example, workers in a factory could be salaried or non-salaried. They could also work in an Operations role, or *not* work in an Operations role. These problems can be represented by a simple Venn diagram, as shown below:

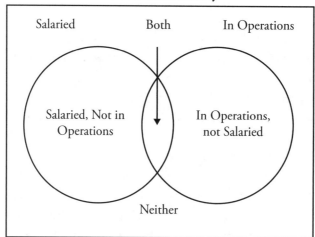

The two key points to note are the following:

1. The workers will *always* fall into one of four groups:

  (a) Salaried and in an Operations role (i.e., "both")
  (b) Salaried and NOT in an Operations role
  (c) NOT salaried and in an Operations role
  (d) NOT salaried and NOT in an Operations role

Therefore, there are four unknowns in this type of problem, generally (although the question itself may only require that you work with two or three of them).

2. The problem will often give you total amounts for the groups (salaried, and in Operations), and you will have to use logic to figure out whichever unknown the question is asking about.

The various sections can be labeled as follows:

Workers in a Factory: <u>Total</u>

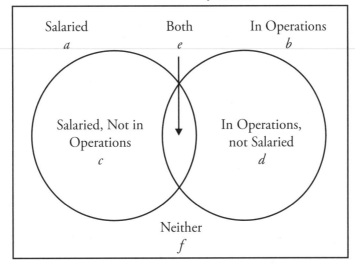

As you can see, $c = a - e$; $d = b - e$, and Total = $a + b - e + f$.

Alternatively, Total = $c + d + e + f$.

Here's an example:

> At Factory X, there are 400 total workers. Of these workers, 240 are salaried, and 220 work in Operations. If at least 100 of the workers are non-salaried and do not work in Operations, what's the minimum number of workers who both are salaried and work in Operations?

Graphically, this looks like:

Workers in a Factory: 400

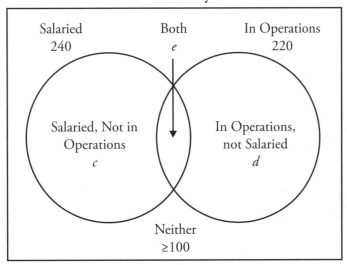

Mathematically, you can use Total = $a + b - e + f$.

$$400 = 240 + 220 - e + (\geq 100)$$

$$e = 240 + 220 - 400 + (\geq 100)$$

$$e = 60 + (\geq 100)$$

$$e = \geq 160$$

Thus, at *least* 160 workers are salaried and work in operations.

Check Your Skills

3. Of 320 consumers, 200 eat strawberries and 300 eat oranges. If all 320 eat at least one of the fruits, how many eat both?

The answer can be found on page 153.

Check Your Skills Answer Key

1. **15:** The group will be as small as possible when everyone contributes as much as they're able to. The most anyone can contribute is $75, so assume that everyone contributes $75:

$$1{,}100 \div 75 = 14\frac{2}{3}$$

However, 14 people contributing $75 would only give $1,050. Therefore, you need to round up. The smallest number of people that could be in the group is 15.

2. **2 cups:** Try the limits. If Oliver used 1 cup of oil, his recipe would require 1/2 cup of vinegar and $1^1/_2$ cups of water. He does not have enough vinegar. If he used 1/3 cup of vinegar, he would need 2/3 cups of oil and 1 cup of water, both of which he has. He would then have 2/3 + 1/3 + 1 = 2 cups of dressing. He cannot possibly make more dressing than this, because he does not have any more vinegar.

3. **180:** Graphically:

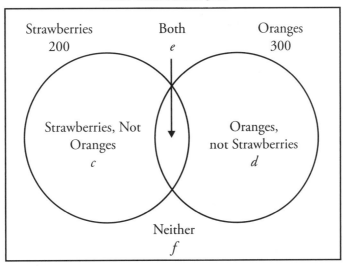

Mathematically, you can use Total = $a + b - e + f$.

Since all of the consumers eat at least one of the fruits, $f = 0$. So:

$$320 = 200 + 300 - e + 0$$
$$320 = 500 - e$$
$$e = 180$$

8

Problem Set

1. Velma has exactly one week to learn all 71 Japanese hiragana characters. If she can learn at most a dozen of them on any one day and will only have time to learn four of them on Friday, what is the least number of hiragana characters that Velma will have to learn on Saturday?

2. Huey's Hip Pizza sells two sizes of square pizzas: a small pizza that measures 10 inches on a side and costs $10, and a large pizza that measures 15 inches on a side and costs $20. If two friends go to Huey's with $30 apiece, how many more square inches of pizza can they buy if they pool their money than if they each purchase pizza alone?

3. An eccentric casino owner decides that his casino should only use chips in $5 and $7 denominations. Which of the following amounts cannot be paid out using these chips?

    (A) $31   (B) $29   (C) $26   (D) $23   (E) $21

4. A "Collector's Coin Set" contains a one-dollar coin, a fifty-cent coin, a quarter (= 25 cents), a dime (= 10 cents), a nickel (= 5 cents), and a penny (= 1 cent). The Coin Sets are sold for the combined face price of the currency. If Colin buys as many Coin Sets as he can with the $25 he has, how much change will Colin have left over?

5. A rock band is holding a concert and selling tickets. All of the tickets will either be premium seating OR allow backstage access after the event. They will sell 1,200 premium seating tickets and 500 that will allow backstage access. If 150 of the tickets will both be premium seating and allow backstage access, how many total tickets will they sell?

6. Susan is writing a novel that will be 950-pages long when finished. She can write 10 pages per day on weekdays and 20 pages per day on weekends.

Quantity A	Quantity B
The least number of consecutive days it will take Susan to finish her novel	75

8

7. Jared has four pennies (1 cent), one nickel (5 cents) and one dime (10 cents).

Quantity A	Quantity B
The number of different cent values that Jared can achieve using one or more of his coins	20

8. A ribbon 40-inches long is to be cut into three pieces, each of whose lengths is a different integer number of inches.

Quantity A	Quantity B
The least possible length, in inches, of the longest piece	15

9. A farmer sells vegetables to 180 different customers. Of these, 90 of them purchase zucchini and 115 of them purchase cauliflower.

Quantity A	Quantity B
The number of customers who purchased both zucchini and cauliflower	The number of customers that purchased neither zucchini nor cauliflower

Solutions

1. **7:** To minimize the number of hiragana that Velma will have to learn on Saturday, consider the extreme case in which she learns *as many* hiragana *as possible* on the other days. She learns 4 on Friday, leaving $71 - 4 = 67$ for the other six days of the week. If Velma learns the maximum of 12 hiragana on the other five days (besides Saturday), then she will have $67 - 5(12) = 7$ left for Saturday.

2. **25 square inches:** First, figure the area of each pizza: the small is 100 square inches, and the large is 225 square inches. If the two friends pool their money, they can buy three large pizzas, which have a total area of 675 square inches. If they buy individually, though, then each friend will have to buy one large pizza and one small pizza, so they will only have a total of $2(100 + 225) = 650$ square inches of pizza.

3. **(D):** This problem is a grouping problem. You have some integer number of 5's and some integer number of 7's. Which of the answer choices cannot be the sum? One efficient way to eliminate choices is first to cross off any multiples of 7 and/or 5; this eliminates choice (E). Now, any other possible sums must have at least one 5 and one 7 in them. So you can subtract off 5's one at a time until you reach a multiple of 7. (It is easier to subtract 5's than 7's, because our number system is base-10.) Choice (A): $31 - 5 = 26$; $26 - 5 = 21$, a multiple of 7; this eliminates (A). (In other words, $31 = 3 \times 7 + 2 \times 5$.) Choice (B): $29 - 5 = 24$; $24 - 5 = 19$; $19 - 5 = 14$, a multiple of 7; this eliminates (B). Choice (C): $26 - 5 = 21$, a multiple of 7; this eliminates (C). So the answer must be choice (D), 23. You can check by successively subtracting 5 and looking for multiples of 7: $23 - 5 = 18$, not a multiple of 7; $18 - 5 = 13$, also not a multiple of 7; $13 - 5 = 8$, not a multiple of 7; and no smaller result will be a multiple of 7 either.

4. **$0.17:** The first step is to compute the value of a complete "Collector's Coin Set": $1.00 + $0.50 + $0.25 + $0.10 + $0.05 + $0.01 = 1.91. Now, you need to divide $1.91 into $25. A natural first move is to multiply by 10: for $19.10, Colin can buy 10 complete sets. Now add $1.91 successively. Colin can buy 11 sets for $21.01, 12 sets for $22.92, and 13 sets for $24.83. There is $0.17 left over.

5. **1,550:** You can use the formula Total $= a + b - e + f$. Since all of the tickets will either be premium seating or allow backstage access, f will equal 0. Therefore:

    Total $= 1,200 + 500 - 150 = 1,550$

6. **(B):** In a week consisting of 5 workdays and 2 weekend days, Susan can write:

    $5 \times 10 + 2 \times 20 = 90$ pages

Therefore, in 10 consecutive full weeks (i.e., 70 consecutive days), she can write 900 pages of her novel, leaving another 50 pages to be written. The least number of days it would take Susan to write 50 pages is 3: 2 weekend days and 1 weekday. Thus, it is possible for Susan to finish her novel in 73 days. (This assumes that Susan chooses her start day appropriately, so as to take advantage of as many weekends as possible.) Therefore, **Quantity B is greater**.

7. **(B):** Jared can achieve any amount from 1 cent to 19 cents: 1 to 4 cents using the pennies, 5 cents with the nickel, 6 to 9 cents using the nickel along with the pennies, 10 cents using the dime, 11 to 14 cents

using the dime along with the pennies, 15 cents using the dime and the nickel, and 16 to 19 cents using the dime and nickel along with the pennies. Notice that 19 cents requires every coin Jared possesses, meaning that 19 is the largest possible value. That makes 19 possible values. Therefore, **Quantity B is greater**.

8.   **(C):** Minimizing the length of the longest piece is equivalent to maximizing the lengths of the remaining pieces, as long as they are shorter than the longest piece. Suppose that the longest piece were 14 inches long (a choice motivated by wanting to be less than the 15 in Quantity B). That would leave $40 - 14 = 26$ inches to be accounted for by the other two pieces.

Because each piece must be a different number of inches long, those pieces cannot each be 13 inches long. This, in turn, implies that one of the two remaining pieces would have to be more than 13 inches long—but then, that piece would be 14 inches long, again violating the constraint that each piece be of a different length. Thus, the longest piece must be at least 15 inches long, and the shorter pieces could then be 12 and 13 inches long, for a total of 40 inches. Thus, **the two quantities are equal**.

9.   **(A):** Once again using the formula Total $= a + b - e + f$:

$$180 = 90 + 115 - e + f$$
$$180 = 205 - e + f$$
$$e - f = 25$$

Therefore, there will be 25 *more* customers that purchased both zucchini and cauliflower than those who purchased neither. Thus, **Quantity A is greater**.

Chapter 9

of
Word Problems

Drill Sets

In This Chapter...

Chapter Review: Drill Sets

Chapter Review: Drill Sets

Drill Set 1

Translate the following statements into equations and/or inequalities.

1. The total amount of money saved equals $2,000.

2. The number of cars is three fewer than the number of trucks.

3. There are twice as many computers as there are printers.

4. John ran twice as far as Maria.

5. There are 35 marbles in the jar, some green and some blue.

6. Container A is three times as big as Container B.

7. One-half of the students are learning French.

8. Max earned one-third of what Jerome earned.

9. The number of people on the team is four less than three times the number of employees.

10. There are 10 more grapes than apples, and one-fourth as many apples as pears.

Drill Set 2

Translate and solve the following problems.

1. There are 5 more computers in the office than employees. If there are 10 employees in the office, how many computers are there?

2. If −5 is 7 more than z, what is z/4?

3. Each player on the team is required to purchase a uniform that costs $25. If there are 20 players on the team, what will be the total cost of the uniforms?

4. There are two trees in the front yard of a school. The trees have a combined height of 60 feet, and the taller tree is 3 times the height of the shorter tree. How high is the shorter tree?

5. A clothing store bought a container of 100 shirts for $20. If the store sold all of the shirts at $0.50 per shirt, what is the store's gross profit on the container?

6. A bag of 60 marbles is separated into two groups. If the first group contains 16 more marbles than the second group, how many marbles are in the larger group?

7. Two parking lots can hold a total of 115 cars. The Green lot can hold 35 fewer cars than the Red lot. How many cars can the Red lot hold?

9

8. At the county fair, two people are competing to see who can eat the most hot dogs. One competitor eats 7 fewer hot dogs than the other competitor. If the competitor who eats fewer hot dogs eats 25 hot dogs, how many hot dogs did the two people eat, combined?

9. Bansi and Sade ran a combined 30 kilometers. Bansi ran 8 kilometers fewer than Sade did. How many kilometers did Bansi run?

10. A class went to a donut shop, where 13 of the students ate 3 donuts each. The remaining 7 students were hungrier, and ate 8 donuts each. How many total donuts did the class eat?

11. Three friends sit down to eat 14 slices of pizza. If two of the friends eat the same number of slices, and the third eats two more slices than each of the other two, how many slices are eaten by the third friend?

12. A plane leaves Chicago in the morning, and makes three flights before returning. The first flight traveled twice as far as the second flight, and the second flight traveled three times as far as the third flight. If the third flight was 45 miles, how many miles was the first flight?

13. A rubber ball is thrown and bounces twice before it is caught. The first time the ball bounces, it goes 5 times as high as the second time it bounces. If the second bounce goes 5 feet high, what is the combined height of the two bounces?

14. A museum tour guide can take 1 class through a museum in 30 minutes. If all classes have 30 students, how many students could go through the museum in 2 hours?

15. A band on a concert tour played 10 concerts. The first concert attracted 100 people, and the last concert attracted 6 times as many people. If the sixth concert attracted 1/2 as many people as the last concert, how many people were at the sixth concert?

16. Movie theater X charges $6 per ticket, and each movie showing costs the theatre $1,750. If 300 people bought tickets for a certain showing, and the theater averaged $2 in concessions (popcorn, etc.) per ticket holder, what was the theater's profit for that showing?

17. Three health clubs are competing to attract new members. One company runs an ad campaign and recruits 120 new members. The second company runs a similar campaign and recruits 2/3 as many members. The third company recruits 10 more members than the second company. How many new members are recruited by the three companies combined?

18. It costs a certain bicycle factory $10,000 to operate for one month, plus $300 for each bicycle produced during the month. Each of the bicycles sells for a retail price of $700. The gross profit of the factory is measured by total income from sales minus the overall production costs of the bicycles. If 50 bicycles are produced and sold during the month, what is the factory's gross profit?

19. If a harbor cruise can shuttle 50 people per trip, and each trip takes 3 hours, how long will it take for 350 people to complete the tour?

20. Alfred and Nevin cooked a total of 49 pies. If twice the number of pies that Alfred cooked was 14 pies more than the number of pies that Nevin cooked, how many pies did Alfred cook?

21. Arnaldo earns $11 for each ticket that he sells, and a bonus of $2 per ticket for each ticket he sells over 100. If Arnaldo was paid $2,400, how many tickets did he sell?

22. Alicia is producing a magazine that costs $3 per magazine to print. In addition, she has to pay $10,500 to her staff to design the issue. If Alicia sells each magazine for $10, how many magazines must she sell to break even?

23. Eleanor's football team has won 3 times as many games as Christina's football team. Christina's football team has won 4 fewer games than Joanna's team. If Joanna's team won 10 games last year, how many games did Eleanor's team win?

24. The distance between Town X and Town Y is twice the distance between Town X and Town Z. The distance between Town Z and Town W is 2/3 the distance between Town Z and Town X. If the distance between Town Z and Town W is 18 miles, how far is Town X from Town Y?

25. Every week, Renee is paid 40 dollars per hour for the first 40 hours she works, and 80 dollars per hour for each hour she works after the first 40 hours. If she earned $2,000 last week, how many hours did she work?

Drill Set 3

Translate and solve the following word problems involving age.

1. Norman is 12 years older than Malik. In 6 years, he will be twice as old as Malik. How old is Norman now?

2. Louise is three times as old as Mari. In 5 years, Louise will be twice as old as Mari. How old is Mari now?

3. Chris is 14 years younger than Sam. In 3 years, Sam will be 3 times as old as Chris. How old is Sam now?

4. Toshi is 7 years older than his brother Kosuke, who is twice as old as their younger sister Junko. If Junko is 8 years old, how old is Toshi?

5. Amar is 30 years younger than Lauri. In 5 years, Lauri will be three times as old as Amar. How old will Lauri be in 10 years?

9

Translate and solve the following Word Problems involving averages. For the purpose of these problems "average" means the arithmetic mean.

Remember that $A = \dfrac{S}{n}$, where A = average, n = the number of terms, and S = the sum of the terms.

6. Three lawyers earn an average of $300 per hour. How much money have they earned in total after they each worked 4 hours?

7. The average of 2, 13, and x is 10. What is x?

8. Last year, Nancy earned twice the amount of money that Janet earned. Kate earned three times the amount Janet earned. If Kate earned $45,000 last year, what was the average salary of the three women?

9. Tari buys 5 books with an average price of $12. If Tari then buys another book with a price of $18, what is the average price of the six books?

10. If the average of the five numbers $x - 3$, x, $x + 3$, $x + 4$, and $x + 11$ is 45, what is the value of x?

Translate and solve the following Word Problems involving Rates. Remember that $RT = D$, where R = rate, T = time, and D = distance.

11. Bay drove to the store at a rate of 30 miles per hour. If the store is 90 miles away, how long did it take him to get there?

12. Maria normally walks at a rate of 4 miles per hour. If she walks at one-half of her normal rate, how long will it take her to walk 4 miles?

13. A train traveled at a constant rate from New York to Chicago in 9 hours. If the distance between New York and Chicago is 630 miles, how fast was the train going?

14. Randy completed a 12-mile run in 4 hours. If Dakota ran 3 miles per hour faster than Randy, how long did it take her to complete the same 12-mile run?

15. A truck uses 1 gallon of gasoline every 15 miles. If the truck travels 3 hours at 60 miles per hour, how many gallons of gasoline will it use?

Drill Set Answers

Drill Set 1

1. $m = \$2{,}000$

2. $c = t - 3$

3. $c = 2p$

4. $j = 2m$ (or $d_j = 2d_m$)

5. $35 = g + b$

6. $A = 3B$

7. $1/2\ S = F$

8. $M = J/3$

9. $t = 3e - 4$

10. $g = a + 10$
    $a = 1/4\ p$

Drill Set 2

1. **15 computers:** Let c = number of computers.
    Let e = number of employees.

    $c = e + 5$

    If $e = 10$, then $c = (10) + 5$
    $c = 15$

2. **−3:** $-5 = z + 7$
    $z = -12$
    $z/4 = -3$

3. **$500:** Let u = cost of each uniform.
    Let p = number of players.
    Let C = the total cost of the uniforms.

    $C = u \times p$

    If $p = 20$, and $u = \$25$, then $C = (\$25) \times (20) = \$500$

4. **15 feet:** Let s = the height of the shorter tree.
    Let t = the height of the taller tree.

    $s + t = 60$
    $3s = t$

$$s + (3s) = 60$$
$$4s = 60$$
$$s = 15$$

5. **$30:** Let p = profit.

     Let r = revenue.

     Let c = cost.

     Profit = Revenue − Cost
     $$p = r - c$$
     $$r = 100 \times \$0.50$$
     $$c = \$20$$

     $$p = (100 \times \$0.50) - (\$20)$$
     $$p = \$50 - \$20 = \$30$$

6. **38 marbles:** Let f = the number of marbles in the first group.

     Let s = the number of marbles in the second group.

     $$f + s = 60$$
     $$f = s + 16$$
     $$(s + 16) + s = 60$$
     $$2s + 16 = 60$$
     $$2s = 44$$
     $$s = 22$$

     $$f = (22) + 16 = 38$$

7. **75 cars:** Let g = the number of cars that the Green lot can hold.

     Let r = the number of cars that the Red lot can hold.

     $$g + r = 115$$
     $$g = r - 35$$

     $$(r - 35) + r = 115$$
     $$2r - 35 = 115$$
     $$2r = 150$$
     $$r = 75$$

     $$g = r - 35 = 75 - 35 = 40$$

     Red lot: 75 cars

     Green lot: 40 cars

8. **57 hot dogs:** Let f = the number of hot dogs eaten by the first competitor (assume he or she ate fewer).

     Let s = the number of hot dogs eaten by the second competitor.

     $$f = s - 7$$
     $$f = 25$$

Therefore,

$(25) = s - 7$

$s = 32$

$25 + 32 = 57$

9. **11 miles:** Let B = the number of miles run by Ben.

   Let S = the number of miles run by Sarah.

   $B + S = 30$

   $B = S - 8$

   $B + 8 = S$

   $B + (B + 8) = 30$

   $2B + 8 = 30$

   $2B = 22$

   $B = 11$

10. **95 donuts:** 13 students ate 3 donuts each: $13 \times 3 = 39$.

    7 students ate 8 donuts each: $7 \times (8) = 56$.

    Total $= 39 + 56 = 95$

11. **6 slices of pizza:** Let P = the number of slices of pizza eaten by each of the two friends who eat the same amount.

    Let T = the number of slices of pizza eaten by the third friend.

    $T = P + 2$

    $P + P + T = 14$

    $P + P + (P + 2) = 14$

    $3P + 2 = 14$

    $3P = 12$

    $P = 4$

    $T = P + 2 = 4 + 2 = 6$

12. **270 miles:** Let F = the distance of the first flight.

    Let S = the distance of the second flight.

    Let T = the distance of the third flight.

    $F = 2S$

    $S = 3T$

    $T = 45$

    $S = 3 \times (45) = 135$

    $F = 2 \times (135) = 270$

9

13. **30 feet:** Let a = the height of the first bounce.
Let b = the height of the second bounce.

$a = 5 \times b$
$b = 5$

$a = 5 \times (5) = 25$

Total height = $a + b = 25 + 5 = 30$

14. **120 students:** If each tour takes 30 minutes, a guide can complete 4 tours in 2 hours.

4 tours × 30 students = 120 students

15. **300 people:** Let f = the number of people at the first concert.
Let l = the number of people at the last concert.
Let s = the number of people at the sixth concert.

$f = 100$
$l = 6f = 6 \times (100) = 600$
$s = 1/2 (l) = 1/2 \times (600) = 300$

16. **$650:** Profit = Revenue − Cost

Revenue = $300 \times 6 + 300 \times 2 = 1{,}800 + 600 = 2{,}400$
Cost = 1,750

Profit = 2,400 − 1,750 = 650

17. **290 new members:** Let a = the number of new members recruited by the first company.
Let b = the number of new members recruited by the second company.
Let c = the number of new members recruited by the third company.

$a = 120$
$b = 2/3 (a) = 2/3 \times (120) = 80$
$c = b + 10 = (80) + 10 = 90$

$a + b + c = 120 + 80 + 90 = 290$

18. **$10,000:** Profit = Revenue − Cost

Revenue = $50 \times 700 = 35{,}000$
Cost = $10{,}000 + (50 \times 300) = 10{,}000 + 15{,}000 = 25{,}000$

Thus, Profit = 35,000 − 25,000 = 10,000.

19. **21 hours:** First, figure out how many trips you need. If each trip can accommodate 50 people, then you will need:

350 people/50 = 7 trips

7 trips × 3 hours = 21 hours

20. **21 pies:** Let A = the number of pies that Alfred cooked.
    Let N = the number of pies that Nevin cooked.

    $A + N = 49$
    $2A = N + 14$
    $2A - 14 = N$

    $A + (2A - 14) = 49$
    $3A - 14 = 49$
    $3A = 63$
    $A = 21$

21. **200 tickets:** Let x = the total number of tickets sold. Therefore, $(x - 100)$ equals the number of tickets sold over 100. Thus:

    $11x + 2(x - 100) = 2{,}400$
    $11x + 2x - 200 = 2{,}400$
    $13x = 2{,}600$
    $x = 200$

22. **1,500 magazines:** Let m = the number of magazines sold.
    Total cost = $3m + 10{,}500$.
    Total revenue = $10m$.

    Breaking even occurs when total revenue equals total cost, so:

    $3m + 10{,}500 = 10m$
    $10{,}500 = 7m$
    $1{,}500 = m$

23. **18 games:** Let E = the number of games Eleanor's team won.
    Let C = the number of games Christine's team won.
    Let J = the number of games Joanna's team won.

    $E = 3C$
    $C = J - 4$
    $J = 10$

    $C = (10) - 4 = 6$
    $E = 3(6) = 18$

24. **54 miles:** Let $[XY]$ = the distance between Town X and Town Y.
    Let $[XZ]$ = the distance between Town X and Town Z.
    Let $[ZW]$ = the distance between Town Z and Town W.

    Translating the information in the question, you get:
    $[XY] = 2[XZ]$ From the first sentence
    $[ZW] = 2/3\ [XZ]$ From the second sentence
    $[ZW] = 18$ From the third sentence

9

$18 = 2/3\ [XZ]$

$54/2 = [XZ]$

$27 = [XZ]$

$[XY] = 2(27) = 54$

25. **45 hours:** Let h = number of hours Renee worked.

$40(40) + (h - 40)(80) = 2{,}000$ assuming $h > 40$

$1{,}600 + 80h - 3{,}200 = 2{,}000$

$80h - 1{,}600 = 2{,}000$

$80h = 3{,}600$

$h = 45$

Drill Set 3

1. **18 years old:** Let N = Norman's age now. $(N + 6)$ = Norman's age in 6 years.
   Let M = Malik's age now. $(M + 6)$ = Malik's age in 6 years.

$N = M + 12$	Translate the first sentence into an equation.
$N + 6 = 2\,(M + 6)$	Translate the second sentence into an equation.
$N - 12 = M$	Rewrite the first equation to put it in terms of M.
$N + 6 = 2(N - 12 + 6)$	Insert $N - 12$ for M in the second equation.
$N + 6 = 2(N - 6)$	
$N + 6 = 2N - 12$	
$18 = N$	Solve for N.

2. **5 years old:** Let L = Louise's age now. $(L + 5)$ = Louise's age 5 years from now.
   Let M = Mari's age now. $(M + 5)$ = Mari's age 5 years from now.

$L = 3M$	Translate the first sentence into an equation.
$(L + 5) = 2(M + 5)$	Translate the second sentence into an equation.
$(3M + 5) = 2(M + 5)$	Insert $3M$ for L in the second equation.
$3M + 5 = 2M + 10$	Make sure you distribute the 2.
$M = 5$	Solve for M.

3. **18 years old:** Let C = Chris's age now. $(C + 3)$ = Chris's age 3 years from now.
   Let S = Sam's age now. $(S + 3)$ = Sam's age 3 years from now.

$C = S - 14$	Translate the first sentence into an equation.
$3(C + 3) = (S + 3)$	Translate the second sentence into an equation.
$3C + 9 = S + 3$	
$3(S - 14) + 9 = S + 3$	Insert $S - 14$ for M in the second equation.
$3S - 42 + 9 = S + 3$	
$3S - 33 = S + 3$	
$2S - 33 = 3$	

9

$$2S = 36$$
$$S = 18 \qquad \text{Solve for } S.$$

4. **23 years old:** Let T = Toshi's age.
   Let K = Kosuke's age.
   Let J = Junko's age.

   $$J = 8$$
   $$B = 2 \times J = 2 \times (8) = 16$$
   $$T = B + 7 = (16) + 7 = 23$$

5. **50 years old:** Let A = Amar's age now. $\qquad (A + 5)$ = Amar's age 5 years from now.
   Let L = Lauri's age now. $\qquad (L + 5)$ = Lauri's age 5 years from now.

   You're looking for Lauri's age in 10 years: $L + 10$

   $$A = L - 30 \qquad\qquad \text{Translate the first sentence into an equation.}$$
   $$L + 5 = 3\,(A + 5) \qquad \text{Translate the second sentence into an equation.}$$

   $$L + 5 = 3(L - 30 + 5) \qquad \text{Insert } L - 30 \text{ for } A \text{ in the second equation.}$$
   $$L + 5 = 3(L - 25)$$
   $$L + 5 = 3L - 75$$
   $$80 = 2L$$
   $$40 = L$$

   Remember, you're looking for Lauri's age in 10 years, thus:

   $$L + 10 = 40 + 10 = 50$$

6. **$3,600:** Each lawyer worked 4 hours, earning $300 per hour. $\qquad 4 \times \$300 = \$1,200$

   There are 3 lawyers. $\qquad\qquad\qquad\qquad\qquad\qquad\qquad \$1,200 \times 3 = \$3,600$

   They earned $3,600 in total.

7. **15:** $A = \dfrac{S}{n}$. Here, $10 = A$, S is the sum of the 3 terms (2, 13, x), and 3 is the number of terms. Thus:

   $$\frac{2 + 13 + x}{3} = 10$$

   $$2 + 13 + x = 30$$

   $$15 + x = 30$$

   $$x = 15$$

8. **$30,000:** Let N = the amount of money Nancy earned.

Let J = the amount of money Janet earned.

Let K = the amount of money Kate earned.

Let A = the average salary.

$N = 2J$
$K = 3J$
$K = \$45,000$

$(\$45,000) = 3J$
$\$15,000 = J$

$N = 2(\$15,000)$
$N = \$30,000$

$$\frac{N + K + J}{3} = A$$

$$A = \frac{\$30,000 + \$15,000 + \$45,000}{3} = \frac{\$90,000}{3} = \$30,000$$

9. **$13:** $\dfrac{\text{Sum}}{\text{Number}} = \text{Average}$

First, you need to know the cost of the 5 books.

Sum = (Average)(Number) = (\$12)(5) = \$60.

Sum of the cost of all 6 books = \$60 + \$18 = \$78.

Number of total books = 6.

$\text{Average} = \dfrac{\$78}{6} = \$13.$

10. **42:** $\dfrac{(x-3) + (x) + (x+3) + (x+4) + (x+11)}{5} = 45$

$\dfrac{5x + 15}{5} = 45$

$x + 3 = 45$
$x = 42$

11. **3 hours:** Let r = rate.

Let t = time.

Let d = distance.

$r \times t = d$
$(30 \text{ m/hr}) \times t = 90 \text{ miles}$
$t = 90/30 = 3 \text{ hours}$

12. **2 hours:** Let r = rate.

   Let t = time.

   Let d = distance.

   r = 4 miles/hr

   $1/2 \times r$ = 2 miles/hr

   d = 4 miles

   $r \times t = d$

   2 miles/hr $\times t$ = 4 miles

   $2t = 4$

   t = 2 hours

13. **70 miles per hour:** $rt = d$

   $r(9 \text{ hours}) = 630 \text{ miles}$

   $r = 70$ miles per hour

14. **2 hours:** r = rate at which Randy ran.

   $r + 3$ = the rate at which Dakota ran.

   12 miles = $r(4 \text{ hours})$

   r = 3 miles per hour

   $12 = (r + 3)(t)$

   $12 = (3 + 3)(t)$

   $12 = 6t$

   $2 = t$

15. **12 gallons:** Let d = distance traveled.

   $d = (60 \text{ mph})(3 \text{ hours}) = 180 \text{ miles}$

   180 miles/15 miles per gallon = 12 gallons

9

Chapter 10

of

Word Problems

Word Problems Practice
Question Sets

In This Chapter...

Easy Practice Question Set

1. Five stand-by passengers are waiting for 3 open seats on an airplane flight. In how many different ways can 3 passengers be arranged in these seats?

    (A) 10
    (B) 15
    (C) 20
    (D) 60
    (E) 125

2. When two fair dice are rolled, what is the probability that at least one of the numbers will be even?

    (A) $\dfrac{1}{4}$

    (B) $\dfrac{1}{3}$

    (C) $\dfrac{1}{2}$

    (D) $\dfrac{2}{3}$

    (E) $\dfrac{3}{4}$

3. 60% of the students in a classroom are girls.

Quantity A	Quantity B
The ratio of boys to girls in the classroom	$\dfrac{3}{5}$

4. A pancake recipe calls for $\dfrac{1}{5}$ cup of sugar for every cup of flour.

Quantity A	Quantity B
Number of cups of sugar in 2 cups of sugar/flour mix	$\dfrac{2}{5}$ cups of sugar

5. A printer can print 12 pages per minute. At that rate, how many *seconds* will the printer require to print 30 pages?

    (A) 2.5
    (B)   30
    (C)   42
    (D) 150
    (E) 360

6. | Quantity A | Quantity B |
    |---|---|
    | The average of 34, 46, 42, 30, 38, and 26 | 36 |

7. What is the range of the set of odd integers between 4 and 40?

    (A) 18
    (B) 20
    (C) 34
    (D) 35
    (E) 36

8. Jared drove 2 hours at an average speed of 50 mph before taking a 1-hour lunch break. He then drove the remaining 270 miles at an average speed of 60 mph. What was the total time for his trip, in hours?

    (A)   2
    (B) 4.5
    (C) 6.5
    (D) 7.5
    (E) 9.5

9. At the Golden Buffet, diners can choose either soup or salad for an appetizer; beef, chicken, fish, or pasta for an entrée; and pie or ice cream for dessert. How many different meals can a diner select, if each meal consists of one appetizer, one entrée, and one dessert at the Golden Buffet?

    ☐ meals

10

MANHATTAN
PREP

10. Jorge has 5 quarters and 3 nickels. If he picks two of these coins at random, what is the probability that both will be quarters?

   (A) $\dfrac{1}{4}$

   (B) $\dfrac{5}{14}$

   (C) $\dfrac{25}{64}$

   (D) $\dfrac{5}{8}$

   (E) $\dfrac{2}{3}$

11. A dressing recipe calls for vinegar and oil to be in the ratio 2 : 3 by volume, and for water and oil to be in the ratio 5 : 7 by volume. If there are no other ingredients in the recipe, which of the following statements must be true?

   Indicate <u>all</u> such statements.

   [A] The dressing will contain more water than vinegar.
   [B] At least 25% of the dressing will be vinegar.
   [C] There will be 3 ounces of water in 9 ounces of dressing.
   [D] If you have equal volumes of each ingredient, the amount of dressing you can mix will be limited by the amount of oil.

12. At a bakery, donuts cost $0.85 each, and bagels cost $1.10 each.

Quantity A	**Quantity B**
The total cost of a dozen donuts and a dozen bagels at the bakery	$24

13. Two candidates, Salvador and Tammy, split the 1,000 votes cast in the election for Student Council President. Which of the following statements, taken individually, are sufficient to determine the number of votes cast for Salvador?

   Indicate <u>all</u> such statements.

   [A] The ratio of Salvador's votes to Tammy's votes was 3 : 2.
   [B] Tammy received 40% of the votes.
   [C] The average of Salvador's votes and Tammy's votes was 500.
   [D] Salvador received 200 more votes than Tammy.

14. A biologist analyzes the number of paramecia visible under a microscope for a collection of protozoa samples. The average number of paramecia visible is 8.1 per sample, and the standard deviation of this measure is 2.4. The distribution of paramecia visible across the samples is approximately normal.

Quantity A	Quantity B
The number of paramecia visible at the 75th Percentile in the distribution of samples	10.5

15. Tom buys oranges and bananas from a local fruit stand. In total he spends $8 and buys 8 pieces of fruit. Bananas are more expensive than oranges.

Quantity A	Quantity B
The cost of 2 oranges	$1

16. Andrew brings $5 to the grocery store to buy candy and gum. Candy costs $0.75 apiece and gum costs $1.25 per pack. What's the maximum number of packs of gum Andrew can buy if he buys at least 2 pieces of candy?

(A) 0
(B) 1
(C) 2
(D) 3
(E) 4

17. Jon can finish a race in exactly 4 hours. Stacy runs at a speed that is 50% faster than Jon's speed.

Quantity A	Quantity B
2.5 hours	The amount of time it will take Stacy to complete the race

18. The detergent required to wash 23 loads of laundry costs $3.60.

Quantity A	Quantity B
$40	The cost, rounded to the nearest cent, of the laundry detergent needed to wash 250 loads of laundry

MANHATTAN
PREP

10

19.   A child must choose from among 5 balloons, each of a different color.

Quantity A	**Quantity B**
The number of combinations of 2 different balloons he can choose	The number of combinations of 3 different balloons he can choose

20. X is the probability that an insurance policy will pay off 100% of the value of a claim, and Y is the probability that an insurance policy will pay off 50% of the value of that claim. No other possible outcomes exist.

Quantity A	**Quantity B**
XY	$X - Y$

10

Easy Practice Question Solutions

1. **(D):** You can solve this problem by using the Anagram method. Five people (call them A through E) will be assigned to seats (designated as *1*, *2*, and *3*), with 2 people left without a seat (designated as *N*):

A	B	C	D	E
1	*2*	*3*	*N*	*N*

The total number of possibilities is the number of arrangements of the "word" *123NN*, which yields the same formula as above: 5 items, so 5!, divided by a factorial for all "repeats." The *N* is listed twice, so the correct expression is $\dfrac{5!}{2!}$.

2. **(E):** Problems of this type (characterized by wording such as "at least") are often most easily solved using the "$1 - x$" shortcut. It is easier to solve for the probability of the event *not* happening, because it is easily defined: both numbers come up odd.

The probability of each number coming up odd is $\dfrac{3}{6}$, which simplies to $\dfrac{1}{2}$. Since the two dice are independent, the probability of both coming up odd is $\dfrac{1}{2} \times \dfrac{1}{2}$, which equals $\dfrac{1}{4}$, so the probability of getting at least one even number is $1 - \dfrac{1}{4}$, which equals $\dfrac{3}{4}$.

3. **(A):** If 60% of the students are girls, then 40% must be boys. Thus, the ratio of boys to girls is $\dfrac{40}{60}$, which simplifies to $\dfrac{2}{3}$, which is about 67% (and thus greater than $\dfrac{3}{5}$, which equals 60%).

Alternatively, you can compare $\dfrac{2}{3}$ to $\dfrac{3}{5}$ by cross-multiplying and comparing the numerators: $\dfrac{2}{3}$ is to $\dfrac{3}{5}$ as 10 is to 9. Therefore, **Quantity A is greater**.

4. **(B):** The ratio of sugar to flour is $\dfrac{1}{5}$ to 1, or 1 to 5. Therefore, the ratio of sugar to flour to combined mix is 1 : 5 : 6. You can now use a proportion to determine the number of cups of sugar in a 2-cup mix: 1 cup of sugar is to 6 cups of mix (this is the general proportion), as *x* cups of sugar are to 2 cups of mix (this proportion is composed of the actual amounts used): $\dfrac{1}{6} = \dfrac{x}{2}$, so 6x = 2 and $x = \dfrac{1}{3}$. The comparison now becomes:

$$\dfrac{1}{3} \qquad\qquad\qquad\qquad \dfrac{2}{5}$$

Thus, **Quantity B is greater**.

5. **(D):** The printer's rate of work is $R = 12$ pages/minute, and the total amount of work is $W = 30$ pages. Using the work equation $R \times T = W$, you can solve for the time: $T = \dfrac{W}{R} = \dfrac{30}{12} = 2\dfrac{1}{2}$ minutes. However, the question asks for the answer in *seconds*. Because there are 60 seconds in each minute, you must multiply 2.5×60 to arrive at the correct answer of 150 seconds.

6. **(C):** When the numbers given in Quantity A are written in ascending order, it can be seen that they are evenly spaced in increments of 4: the set becomes {26, 30, 34, 38, 42, 46}. The average (mean) of an evenly spaced set is the same as its median, which is the middle number. In this case, because the number of terms is even, the median is given by the average of the middle two terms: $\dfrac{34 + 38}{2} = 36$. Thus, **the two quantities are equal**.

7. **(C):** The odd integers in the interval 4 to 40 run from 5 to 39, inclusive. The range of a set is found by subtracting its smallest member from the largest member: $39 - 5 = 34$.

8. **(D):** This problem requires the application of the rate formula, $R \times T = D$. To compute the second part of his drive: $T = \dfrac{D}{R} = \dfrac{270}{60} = 4.5$ hours. He also drove 2 hours before lunch and had a 1-hour lunch break. Thus, the total time for his trip was $4.5 + 2 + 1$, which equals 7.5 hours.

9. **16:** The choices of appetizer, entrée, and dessert are independent of each other. Independent choices multiply. Because there are 2 options for the appetizer, 4 options for the entrée, and 2 options for the dessert, the total number of unique combinations is $2 \times 4 \times 2$, which equals 16.

10. **(B):** You can approach this problem as a "choosing without replacement" problem. First, Jorge will pick one of 8 coins, 5 of which are quarters. The probability of his picking a quarter is therefore $\dfrac{5}{8}$. Now suppose that this indeed happens in his first draw. Then, there will be 7 coins left to choose from, and 4 of them will be quarters. (This is the Domino Effect.) The likelihood of picking a quarter next is now $\dfrac{4}{7}$.

The probability of Jorge picking quarters both times is found by multiplying the individual probabilities of the two successive events: $P = \dfrac{5}{8} \times \dfrac{4}{7} = \dfrac{20}{56}$.

11. **(A), (B), and (D):** You can write the given relationships as $V : O = 2 : 3$ and $W : O = 5 : 7$. In order to combine both expressions into a single overall ratio, you first need to make sure that the common element in the two ratios (namely oil) appears as the same number in both ratios. The least common multiple of 3 and 7 is 21, so if you multiply the first ratio by 7 and the second ratio by 3, you can achieve your goal: $V : O = 14 : 21$ and $W : O = 15 : 21$, such that $V : O : W : \text{Total} = 14 : 21 : 15 : 50$ (note that the 50 in the combined ratio is simply the sum of the preceding numbers).

You can now see that choice (A) is true: water to vinegar is in the ratio $15 : 14$. Choice (B) is also correct: vinegar makes up $\dfrac{14}{50} = 28\%$ of the mixture.

Choice (C) is false, because $\frac{15}{50} = \frac{3}{10}$ or 30%, not $\frac{3}{9}$ or $\frac{1}{3}$.

Finally, choice (D) is also correct because you can see that the item you consume the most of is oil. Therefore, given equal amounts to begin with, you will run out of oil the soonest.

12. **(B):** One option is to calculate the cost of a dozen donuts and a dozen bagels and add them together. The former is $0.85 × 12, which is 10.20 and the latter is $1.10 × 12, which is $13.20, so that the total cost is $10.20 + $13.20, which sums to $23.20. This is best done using the Calculator. Therefore, **Quantity B is greater**.

13. **(A), (B),** and **(D):** Let S stand for the number of votes cast for Salvador. Because the total number of votes was 1,000, the number of votes cast for Tammy must equal 1,000 - S. (Note that you could have defined a second variable T to stand for Tammy's votes, but it is good practice in general to reduce the number of unknowns. Since the problem asks you to determine the number of votes cast for Salvador, you have chosen S as the primary variable and expressed Tammy's votes in terms of S.) In order to be correct, each answer choice must allow you to solve for S.

Choice (A) states that $\frac{S}{1,000-S} = \frac{3}{2}$. S can be solved by cross-multiplying. This is a correct answer.

Choice (B) allows you to solve for S by observing that $1,000 - S = \frac{40}{100} \times 1,000 = 400$. This is a correct answer.

Choice (C) tells you nothing new, because the number of total votes is fixed at 1,000. Therefore, the average of Salvador's votes and Tammy's votes, which is the sum of their votes divided by 2, *has* to equal 500. This is an incorrect answer.

Finally, choice (D) tells you that *S − (1,000 − S) = 200*, which is an equation that you can use to solve for *S*. This is a correct answer.

14. **(B):** The 75th percentile of an approximately normally distributed variable is just shy of 1 standard deviation higher than the mean. (About $\frac{2}{3}$ of all observations fall within 1 standard deviation of the mean, so 1 standard deviation above the mean lies at approximately the 50th + (100) × $\left(\frac{1}{2}\right)\left(\frac{2}{3}\right)$ ≈ 83rd percentile.)

Quantity B is 10.5 − 8.1 = 2.4 units above the mean, or exactly 1 standard deviation above the mean. Therefore, **Quantity B is greater**.

15. **(D):** If $8 purchases 8 pieces of fruit, and bananas are more expensive than oranges, then the cost of a banana is greater than $1, and the cost of an orange is less than $1. However, this is not sufficient information to answer the question. For example, it's possible that Tom bought 6 bananas at $1.20 apiece ($7.20 total), and 2 oranges at $0.40 apiece ($0.80 total). Alternatively, it's possible that Tom bought 6 bananas at $1.10 apiece ($6.60 total), and 2 oranges at $0.70 apiece ($1.40 total). You cannot determine whether 2 oranges cost more or less than $1. Therefore, **the relationship cannot be determined from the information given**.

16. **(C):** If Andrew purchases 2 pieces of candy, he will have $5 - 2 \times \$0.75 = \$3.50$ remaining.

Therefore, $\dfrac{\$3.50}{\$1.25} = \dfrac{350}{125} = \dfrac{70}{25} = \dfrac{14}{5} = 2.8$ packs of gum is then all he can afford to purchase. Since a

fraction/decimal number of packs of gum is impossible to buy, Andrew can only buy 2 packs of gum.

17. **(B):** You can use the Distance Formula to help solve this problem: $D = R \times t$. For Jon, you can

divide by R to get $t = \dfrac{D}{R} = 4$. Furthermore, you know that Stacy runs 50% faster than Jon, So RS = (1

+ 0.5) $\times R = 1.5$R. Plugging this into the equation, you get: $t_S = \dfrac{D}{R_S} = \dfrac{D}{1.5R} = 4\left(\dfrac{1}{1.5}\right) = \dfrac{4}{1.5} = \dfrac{8}{3}$ hours.

This is slightly greater than Quantity A, 2.5 hours. Therefore, **Quantity B is greater**.

18. **(A):** If a $3.60 bottle of laundry detergent can be used to wash 23 loads, then the cost per load of

laundry is $\dfrac{\$3.60}{23} \approx \$0.1565$. Notice that the answer hasn't been rounded to the nearest cent yet; do so only

at the end. The cost of 250 loads of laundry is approximately $250 \times \$0.1565 = \$39.13$.

Thus, **Quantity A is greater**.

This calculation can be made almost precisely by using the Calculator.

19. **(C):** The number of ways that a child can choose a set of 2 balloons out of 5 is given by (5 Choose 2):

$\dfrac{5!}{3! \times 2!} = 10$ different possible sets. Similarly, the number of ways that a child can choose a set of 3 bal-

loons out of 5 is given by (5 Choose 3): $\dfrac{5!}{2! \times 3!} = 10$ different possible sets. Thus, **the two quantities
are equal**.

At first the fact that these two quantities are equal may seem surprising. However, upon further inspection, you can see that choosing 2 balloons out of 5 is the same as choosing 3 balloons out of 5: when you choose 2 items out of 5, you are simultaneously choosing to *exclude* 3 items from your choice. You are effectively dividing the 5 balloons into a "Yes" pool and a "No" pool. The second scenario is the reverse of this: you are saying "Yes" to 3 balloons and "No" to 2 balloons. There are the *same number of ways* to say "Yes" to 2 balloons out of 5 as there are to say "No" to 2 balloons out of 5.

20. **(D):** The only constraints given in the problem are that the probabilities X and Y must sum to 1, because no other possible outcomes exist. However, nothing more is known about the relative size of X and Y. For example, if $X = 0.4$, then $Y = 0.6$ and XY is positive while $X - Y$ is negative. By contrast, if $X = 0.8$, then $Y = 0.2$, $XY = 0.16$, and $X - Y = 0.6$. Therefore, either quantity could be greater. Thus, **the relationship cannot be determined from the information given**.

Be careful not to confuse the percentage of the value of a claim that the insurance company will pay with the probability that the insurance company will pay that percentage

10

Medium Practice Question Set

1. Jared will pick 3 friends to join him on a road trip. His friend group consists of 4 musicians and 3 poets. In how many different ways can Jared select his 3 traveling companions so that he has at least one musician and at least one poet among them?

    (A) 16
    (B) 18
    (C) 30
    (D) 36
    (E) 84

2. A car gets 18 miles per gallon of gasoline in city driving and 24 miles per gallon on the highway. Gasoline costs $3 per gallon.

Quantity A	**Quantity B**
The minimum possible fuel cost of driving 420 miles	$50

3. The five offensive linemen on a football team weigh 295, 310, 304, 321, and 298 pounds, respectively. When the heaviest lineman is injured and replaced by a teammate, the average weight of the five linemen drops by 2 pounds. What is the range of the weights of the new group of five linemen?

    (A) 10
    (B) 15
    (C) 16
    (D) 24
    (E) 26

4. Towns X and Y are 220 miles apart along a road. Car A, traveling at 20 miles per hour, leaves from Town X towards Town Y at the same time as Car B, traveling at 35 miles per hour, leaves Town Y towards Town X. How many miles will Car B have traveled when the two cars pass by each other?

    (A) 55
    (B) 70
    (C) 80
    (D) 110
    (E) 140

5. The average weight of the men in a meeting room is 170 pounds and the average
    weight of the women is 130 pounds. If more than 60% of the people in the room are
    men, which of the following could be the average weight of all people in the room?

    Indicate all such average weights.

    [A] 144
    [B] 148
    [C] 150
    [D] 152
    [E] 154
    [F] 156
    [G] 158
    [H] 168

6.

Score	64	70	72	79	83	85	90	94	95
Number of students achieving that score	1	2	1	4	4	2	3	2	1

    The frequency distribution of student scores on a test is as shown above. How many
    of the scores are above the class average?

    [   ] scores

7. Two journalists have 8 hours in which to copy edit a total of 100 articles. If Journalist
    A copy edits at a steady rate of 3.5 articles per hour, how many articles per hour must
    Journalist B copy edit in order to complete the assignment on time?

    (A) 12.5
    (B) 9
    (C) 8
    (D) 4.5
    (E) 3

8. The ratio of violinists to cellists at a conservatory is 3 to 1. If 180 of the violinists
    depart, and all the cellists remain, the result is a new ratio of 3 violinists to 2 cellists.
    How many cellists are enrolled at the conservatory?

    [   ] cellists

9. The ratio of boys to girls in a certain coed school is greater than 1. When 2 boys leave and 3 girls are added to the school, the ratio still favors boys. What is the least number of boys that could have been originally enrolled in the school, assuming there was originally *at least* one girl?

    (A) 1
    (B) 4
    (C) 6
    (D) 7
    (E) 13

10.

Asset	Amount Invested	Expected Return
Stock X	$40	10%
Stock Y	$40	8%
Stock Z	$20	15%

Quantity A	**Quantity B**
The percent return an investor would expect for investing the amounts listed in the stocks above	10.5%

11. Roger bought some pencils and erasers at the stationery store. If he bought more pencils than erasers, and the total number of the pencils and erasers he bought is between 12 and 20 (inclusive), which of the following statements must be true?

    Indicate all such statements.

    [A] Roger bought no fewer than 7 pencils.
    [B] Roger bought no more than 12 pencils.
    [C] Roger bought no fewer than 6 erasers.
    [D] Roger bought no more than 9 erasers.

12. At an event, 40% of the attendees are over 50 years old and another 20% are under 20 years old. Which of the following statements must be true?

    Indicate all such statements.

    [A] The ratio of those over 50 to those between 20 and 50 inclusive is 2 : 3.
    [B] The ratio of those under 20 to those between 20 and 50 inclusive is 1 : 2.
    [C] $\frac{1}{3}$ of the attendees who are not over 50 are under 20.
    [D] There are at least 10 attendees.

MANHATTAN
PREP

13. Five years ago, Abigail was half as old as Benji. Next year the sum of their ages will be 27.

Quantity A	Quantity B
Abigail's age next year	Benji's age 5 years ago

14. Set X consists of 100 bags of rice with an average weight of 90 pounds per bag, and the standard deviation of the weights is 8 pounds. The weight of Bag A is 2 standard deviations below the average weight of the bags in set X. Bag B weighs 5 pounds more than the average weight of set X.

Quantity A	Quantity B
Twice the difference between the weight of Bag B and the weight of Bag A	The range of weights of the bags of rice in set X

15. The probability of rainfall in City *X* on any given day is 30%. The probability of rainfall on any given day is independent of whether it rains on any other day.

Quantity A	Quantity B
The probability of rainfall in City *X* on *at least* one day out of two days	The probability of no rainfall in City *X* on either of those two days

16. State Y charges a 4% tax on all residential household telephone lines each month, rounded to the nearest penny. Customer A spends less than $50 each month on his telephone bill, including tax.

Quantity A	Quantity B
$48	The cost of Customer A's telephone bill *before* tax

17. Jennifer can purchase 11-cent and 21-cent stamps. If she intends to spend *exactly* $2.84 on these stamps, which of the following is a possible number of 11-cent stamps she can purchase?

(A) 0
(B) 1
(C) 2
(D) 3
(E) 4

18.

Total Consumers Polled: 305

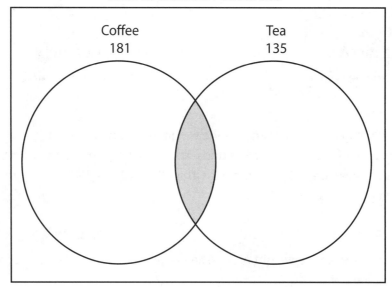

In a sample of 305 consumers polled, 181 drink coffee, and 135 drink tea. The grey area in the Venn diagram represents the consumers who drink both.

Quantity A	**Quantity B**
The number of consumers polled who consume *both* coffee and tea	The number of consumers polled who consume *neither* coffee nor tea

19. In a recreation club with 212 members, 130 participate in kickboxing and 110 participate in rowing. If at least 10% of the club's members participate in neither kickboxing nor rowing, what's the minimum number of members who participate in both?

20. A pomegranate grower packages pomegranates in 10-pound and 20-pound boxes. If the grower fills more than twice as many 20-pound boxes as 10-pound boxes, which of the following could be the percentage of pomegranates, by weight, that are packaged in 10-pound boxes?

(A) 15%

(B) 20%

(C) 25%

(D) 40%

(E) 60%

Medium Practice Question Solutions

1. **(C):** Jared has to select either 2 musicians and 1 poet, or 1 musician and 2 poets. The number of ways he can select 2 musicians from among 4 is given by $\frac{4!}{2!\times 2!} = \frac{24}{4} = 6$, while the number of ways to select 1 poet from among 3 is 3. Thus, there are $6 \times 3 = 18$ ways to select 2 musicians and 1 poet. Similarly, the number of ways to select 2 poets out of 3 is $\frac{3!}{2!\times 1!} = \frac{6}{2} = 3$, while the number of ways to select 1 musician from among 4 is 4. This gives Jared another $4 \times 3 = 12$ ways to select his traveling companions. The total number of options Jared has is $18 + 12$, which is 30.

2. **(A):** In order to incur the least possible cost in fuel, the car must be driven on the highway for the entire 420 miles, so that the higher mile per gallon figure applies. The number of gallons of fuel required for the trip is given by $\frac{420}{24} = \frac{35}{2} = 17\frac{1}{2}$ gallons. The cost of the fuel is $3 times this minimum number of gallons:

The minimum possible fuel cost of driving 420 miles =

Quantity A	**Quantity B**
$\$3 \times 17\frac{1}{2} = \$52\frac{1}{2}$	$\$50$

Therefore, **Quantity A is greater**.

3. **(C):** If the replacement of one player by another lowers the average weight by 2 pounds, you can conclude that the sum of the 5 weights must have dropped by 2×5, which equals 10. This is because the average equals the sum divided by the number of terms.

Based on the 10-pound drop in total weight, you can further conclude that the heaviest lineman, who weighed 321 pounds, must have been replaced by a teammate who weighs 311 pounds and is now the heaviest of the group. The range of weights is found by subtracting the weight of the lightest lineman (295 pounds) from 311: $311 - 295 = 16$.

4. **(E):** One way to solve this problem is to use an *RTD* chart, as shown below:

Car	R (miles/hour)	T (hours)	D (miles)
A	20	t	$20t$
B	35	t	$35t$

The times for the two cars are equal, because they start simultaneously. The sum of the distances traveled by the two cars must equal 220 miles. You can solve for t: $20t + 35t = 55t = 220$, so $t = 4$ hours. The distance traveled by Car B is then found as follows: $R \times t = 35 \times 4 = 140$ miles.

10

An alternative method would be to add the rates of the two cars, since they are traveling towards each other. The combined rate of 55 miles per hour is the rate at which the initial distance of 220 miles shrinks to zero. This will also lead to $t = 4$ hours.

Yet another approach is to tabulate the distances traveled by the two cars every hour, continuing until the total distance equals 220 miles.

5.   **(F)**, **(G)**, and **(H)**: This problem can be solved as a Weighted Average problem. The overall average weight will be between 130 and 170 pounds, but closer to 170 pounds because there are more men than women in the room. You can use the limiting percentage of 60 to establish the lower bound on the overall average weight: if the percentage of men is greater than 60, then the result will be higher than this lower bound. The "weights" to use in the Weighted Average formula are 60%, or $\frac{3}{5}$, for the men and 40%, or $\frac{2}{5}$, for the women. The lower bound on the average weight is thus:

$\frac{3}{5} \times 170 + \frac{2}{5} \times 130 = 102 + 52 = 154$ pounds. This value is not possible, because the percentage of men is greater than 60; however, all the values greater than 154 are possible.

6.   **12**: The total number of student test scores is found by adding the numbers in the second row; the result is 20. You can find the average score by dividing the sum of all scores by 20. The sum of all scores is best found using the memory function of the calculator. First, make sure that the memory is clear by pressing MC. Then, multiply each score by its frequency and add the result to the running sum in memory: $64 \times 1 = M+$, $70 \times 2 = M+$, etc., up to $95 \times 1 = M+$. At that point, retrieve the sum from memory using MR (the result is 1,647) and divide by 20 to obtain 82.35 as the average score. Finally, from the table, add up the number of students who scored 83 and above to obtain the final answer of 12.

7.   **(B)**: In order to find Journalist A's work, you must multiply rate by time: $R \times t = W = 3.5$ articles per hour $\times$ 8 hours = 28 articles. Journalist B must therefore copy edit $100 - 28 = 72$ articles.

To find Journalist B's rate, simply plug 72 for Work into the work formula and solve for B's rate: $R_B \times 8$ hours = 72, so R_B equals 9 articles per hour.

Alternatively, since the journalists are working on the same task over the same time interval, you can combine their rates:

$(R_A + R_B) \times 8$ hours = 100

$(R_A + R_B) = 12.5$

$(3.5 + R_B) = 12.5$

$R_B = 9$

8. **120**: The original ratio can be expressed in a proportion equation:

$\frac{v}{c} = \frac{3}{1}$

$v = 3c$

After the departure of 180 violinists, you have a new proportion:

$$\frac{v-180}{c}=\frac{3}{2}$$

You now have two equations and two variables and can combine and solve. Since you are solving for c, you should simplify and substitute for v first:

$$\frac{v-180}{c}=\frac{3}{2}$$
$$2(v-180)=3c$$
$$2v-360=3c$$
$$2(3c)-360=3c$$
$$3c=360$$
$$c=120$$

Therefore, there are 120 cellists.

You might also notice that when the 180 violinists depart, the ratio of violinists to cellists is cut in half. Therefore, 180 must have been half of the violinists. Originally, then, there must have been 360 violinists. Since there were 3 times as many violinists as cellists, there were $\frac{360}{3}=120$ cellists.

9.   **(D):** Because the ratio of boys to girls is greater than 1, you know that there are more boys than girls in this school:

$$b>g$$

When 2 boys leave and 3 girls are added, the ratio is still greater than 1: $\frac{b-2}{g+3}>1$.

Solve for b:

$$b-2>g+3$$
$$b>g+5$$

Because you want to minimize b, choose g to be as small as possible. The school is coed and the boy/girl ratio is greater than 1, so the smallest number of girl students is 1. Thus, choose $g=1$ to yield $b>6$. Therefore, the least number of boys that could have been originally enrolled in the school is 7. Checking, note that with 7 boys and 1 girl originally enrolled in the school, and when 2 boys leave and 3 girls are added, the new ratio is $\frac{5}{4}$, which is greater than 1.

10. **(B):** The investor invests $100 total. The Weighted Average formula states that the expected return would be equal to (percent invested in X)(expected return of X) + (percent invested in Y)(expected return of Y) + (percent invested in Z)(expected return of Z). Hence, the expected return would be:
(40%)(10%) + (40%)(8%) + (20%)(15%) = (4%) + (3.2%) + (3%) = 10.2%.

10

MANHATTAN
PREP

If you choose to use the calculator, you would enter $(0.4 \times 10) + (0.4 \times 8) + (0.2 \times 15)$ to yield 10.2. To store the products along the way, use the M+ or MR keys.

Quantity A	**Quantity B**
10.2%	10.5%

Therefore, **Quantity B is greater**.

11. **(A)** and **(D)**: Choice (A) is true because Roger would have bought at least 7 pencils (to go with 5 erasers) if he bought the minimum possible total number of items. (6 of each is impossible, as the number of pencils is greater than the number of erasers. Likewise, choice (C) is disproved, as the number of erasers would have been fewer than 6 in this case.) If he bought more than 12 items, the number of pencils could not be any less than 7 and still be greater than the number of erasers.

On the other hand, choice (B) need not be true, because Roger could have bought as many as 19 pencils, even if you assume that he has to buy at least one of each item.

Finally, choice (D) must be true, because even if Roger bought the maximum possible number of items (20), less than half of those would have to be erasers. Thus, 9 erasers is the most he could have purchased; 10 of each is impossible.

12. **(B)** and **(C)**: You can see that $100\% - 40\% - 20\% = 40\%$ of the attendees are between 20 and 50 years old. Thus, choice (A) is not true; the real ratio is $40 : 40 = 1 : 1$. On the other hand, choice (B) is true, because $20 : 40 = 1 : 2$. Choice (C) is also true, because 60% of the attendees are not over 50, and of those, 20% (or $\frac{1}{3}$ of 60%) are under 20.

Choice (D) requires a little more thinking. There is a hidden constraint in the problem because the number of attendees must be an integer. Expressed as fractions, the percentages of those over 50, between 20 and 50, and under 20 are $\frac{2}{5}, \frac{2}{5}$, and $\frac{1}{5}$, respectively. This means that the total number of attendees has to be divisible by 5. The smallest such number is 5. Thus, choice (D) is not necessarily true.

13. **(A)**: First, assign variables:

a = Abigail's age NOW

b = Benji's age NOW

Next, translate the given equations:

(1) $(a - 5) = (1/2)(b - 5)$

(2) $(a + 1) + (b + 1) = 27$

Now you can solve by simplifying these equations and substituting:

(1) $2(a - 5) = b - 5$

$2a - 10 = b - 5$

$2a - 5 = b$

(2) $a + b + 2 = 27$

$a + b = 25$

Substitute (1) into (2) and solve for a:

$a + (2a - 5) = 25$

$3a - 5 = 25$

$3a = 30$

$a = 10$

Now plug a back in to (2) (you could also plug into (1)) and solve for b:

$10 + b = 25$

$b = 15$

Abigail next year will be one year older than Benji was 5 years ago. Thus, **Quantity A is greater**.

14. **(D):** The information in the problem relates the weights of Bag A and Bag B to the average weight of the bags in the sample. Since Bag A is 2 standard deviations below normal weight, its weight is $90 - 2 \times 8 = 74$ pounds, and the difference between the weight of Bag B versus that of Bag A is $(90 + 5) - 74 = 95 - 74 = 21$ pounds. Thus, twice that difference is 42 pounds.

The range of the weight of the bags in set X could be less than, more than, or equal to 42. Dividing by the standard deviation, this implies a range equivalent to $\frac{42}{8} = 5.25$ standard deviations, which would be a large standardized range for a sample, but it's possible that the actual range is greater than that. Thus, **the relationship cannot be determined from the information given**.

10

15. **(A):** The probability of rainfall on at least one of the two days is equal to P(Rain 1st day) + P(Rain 2nd day) − P(Rain both days), since rainfall on each day is independent of what happened on other days. This probability equals: $0.3 + 0.3 − (0.3 × 0.3) = 0.6 − 0.09 = 0.51$ or 51%.

Alternatively, you can use the "$1 − x$" trick here: the probability of rainfall on at least one of the two days is 1 − the probability of rain on neither day (0.7^2). Therefore, the probability is $1 − 0.7 × 0.7 = 1 − 0.49 = 0.51 = 51\%$.

Quantity B, the probability of no rainfall on either day, follows from the work above: $0.7 × 0.7 = 0.49$, which is 49%.

Thus, **Quantity A is greater**.

16. **(D):** The total value of the bill is equal to the original value of the bill, plus 4% of that original value. To use algebra, $T = O + 0.04O = 1.04O$, where O is the original value of the bill (pre-taxes) and T is the total cost of the bill (including taxes).

The question states that for Customer A, T < 50. Therefore, $1.04O < 50$, and $O < \dfrac{\$50}{1.04} \approx \$48.07$.

Therefore, the original bill could have cost $48.07 (tax of $1.92), or $48 (tax of $1.92), or $30 (tax of $1.20). Thus, **the relationship cannot be determined from the information given**.

17. **(B):** 11 and 21 are relatively prime numbers (meaning, they do not share any prime factors in common). Therefore, it is more likely that only a few possible combinations of 11-cent and 21-cent stamps will add up to exactly $2.84. The easiest way to test this is to try each of the choices, and see whether the remaining money (after buying the given number of 11-cent stamps) results in exactly the right amount of money to buy some integer number of 21-cent stamps:

Number of 11-cent Stamps	Cash Remaining After Purchasing 11-cent Stamps	Number of 21-cent Stamps (nearest hundredth)
0	$2.84	13.52 (INCORRECT)
1	**$2.73**	**13 (CORRECT)**
2	$2.62	12.48 (INCORRECT)
3	$2.51	11.95 (INCORRECT)
4	$2.40	11.43 (INCORRECT)

It can be shown, incidentally, that the only other combination that works is to purchase twenty-two 11-cent stamps ($2.42) and two 21-cent stamps ($0.42).

MANHATTAN
PREP

18. **(A):** The number of coffee drinkers plus the number of tea drinkers is equal to 181 + 135, which sums to 316. Because there are only a total of 305 consumers who were surveyed, at least 316 − 305 = 11 consumers must consume both. Thus, in the case where everyone polled drank at least one of the two beverages, there were 11 more consumers of both beverages than of neither beverage. To take the other extreme, assume all 135 tea drinkers also drink coffee. Then, 305 − 181 = 124 consumers would drink neither of the beverages—versus 135 who drank both. Once again, the "both" category exceeds the "neither" category by 11.

In fact, this difference of 11 will be constant irrespective of how many consumers fall into the "both" category:

(coffee drinkers + tea drinkers − drinkers of both) + drinkers of neither = 305

(181 + 135 − drinkers of both) + drinkers of neither = 305

316 − drinkers of both + drinkers of neither = 305

drinkers of both − drinkers of neither = 11

Thus, Quantity A will always be 11 greater than Quantity B. Therefore, **Quantity A is greater**.

19. **50:** At least 10% of the recreation club participates in neither kickboxing nor rowing. Therefore, at least 10%(212) = 21.2 people are in neither activity. Since only integer numbers of members can exist, at least 22 members must not participate in either activity. You can draw a Venn diagram to illustrate this problem:

Total Members: 212

Kickboxing 130   Both ?   Rowing 110   Neither ≥ 22

For the "Neither" category to reach ≥ 22, the kickboxing and rowing circles have to include no more than 212 – ≥22 = ≤190 members. Thus, since there are 130 + 110 = 240 "memberships" in the kickboxing and rowing activities combined, there has to be an "overlap" of at least 50 members in both activities to balance the diagram out:

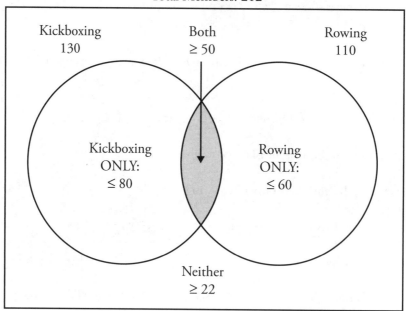

Total Members: 212

Kickboxing 130   Both ≥ 50   Rowing 110

Kickboxing ONLY: ≤ 80

Rowing ONLY: ≤ 60

Neither ≥ 22

Thus, in the scenario where exactly 50 members are involved in both kickboxing and rowing, there are 80 members involved in kickboxing only, 60 involved in rowing only, and 22 involved in neither. Thus, 50 + 80 + 60 + 22 sums to 212, so the goal has been achieved.

20. **(A):** If the grower produces more than twice as many 20-pound boxes as 10-pound boxes, then more than $\frac{2}{3}$ of the boxes will be 20-pound boxes. Therefore, less than $\frac{1}{3}$ of the boxes will be 10-pound boxes.

Furthermore, each 20-pound box contains twice as much fruit, by weight, as does a 10-pound box. Therefore, for every pound of pomegranates packaged in 10-pound boxes, more than (2)(2) = 4 pounds will come from 20-pound boxes. This means that less than $\frac{1}{1+(2)(2)} = \frac{1}{5}$, or 20%, of the weight of the packaged pomegranates comes from 10-pound boxes. Only choice (A) is less than 20%.

For a numerical example, assume there are ten 10-pound boxes filled. Then, at least twenty-one 20-pound boxes must be filled. Assuming these numbers, 10 × 10 = 100 pounds of pomegranates come from 10-pound boxes, and 21 × 20 = 420 pounds come from 20-pound boxes. Thus, only

$\frac{100}{100+420} = \frac{100}{520} \approx 19.23\%$ of the weight of pomegranates comes from 10-pound boxes.

Hard Practice Question Set

CAUTION: These problems are *very difficult*—more difficult than many of the problems you will likely see on the GRE. Consider these "Challenge Problems." Have fun!

1. A steel bar 135 inches long will be cut into a number of 5-inch and 7-inch segments, with no part of the original steel bar left over.

Quantity A	**Quantity B**
The minimum possible number of 5-inch pieces	5

2. A drawer contains 6 brown socks and 4 black socks. What is the probability that the first two socks pulled from the drawer will be of the same color?

    (A) $\dfrac{1}{3}$

    (B) $\dfrac{7}{15}$

    (C) $\dfrac{1}{2}$

    (D) $\dfrac{8}{15}$

    (E) $\dfrac{2}{3}$

3. Four people each roll a fair die once.

Quantity A	**Quantity B**
The probability that *at least* two people will roll the same number	70%

4. A company employs 20 workers for every 3 managers, and 5 managers for every director. If the total number of employees at the company is between 300 and 400, what is the number of managers who work at the company?

    [ ] managers

5. A set of integers consists of 2, 3, 5, 7, 11, 12, and x. If x increases by 1, the median of the set stays unchanged. However, if x decreases by 1, the median of the set also decreases by 1. What is the value of x?

    [ ]

10

6. Jaya can flip 40 pancakes per minute, whereas Sally works at half Jaya's rate. How many minutes will it take the two of them to flip 150 pancakes, if Sally flips the first 30 by herself and is then joined by Jaya for the remainder?

Give your answer as a decimal: ☐

7. Jake rides his bike for the first $\frac{2}{3}$ of the distance from home to school, traveling at 10 miles per hour. He then walks the remaining $\frac{1}{3}$ of the distance at 3 miles per hour. If his total trip takes 40 minutes, how many miles is it from Jake's home to his school?

(A) $\frac{5}{4}$

(B) $\frac{15}{4}$

(C) 5

(D) 6

(E) 10

8. Jasper is to select a committee of 4 individuals from among a group of 5 candidates. The committee will have a President, a Vice President, and two Treasurers. How many different committees can John select from the 5 candidates?

☐ committees

9. Frank is organizing a charity event in an effort to raise money to build a neighborhood park. The park will cost $1,200 to build. Each person attending the event will donate $300, less $20 for each person who attends the event. Thus, for example, if 3 people attend the event, each person will donate $300 − $20(3) = $240. What is the minimum number of people who must attend the event in order to raise enough money to build the park?

(A) 4

(B) 5

(C) 6

(D) 8

(E) Frank cannot raise enough money at this charity event to build the park.

10. Country X has three coins in its currency: a *duom* worth 2 cents, a *trippim* worth 11 cents, and a *megam* worth 19 cents. If a man has $3.21 worth of Country X's currency and cannot carry more than 20 coins, what is the least number of *trippim* he could have?

    (A) 0
    (B) 1
    (C) 2
    (D) 3
    (E) It cannot be determined.

11. In a certain class, $\frac{1}{5}$ of the boys are shorter than the shortest girl in the class, and $\frac{1}{3}$ of the girls are taller than the tallest boy in the class. If there are 16 students in the class and no two people have the same height, what percent of the students are taller than the shortest girl and shorter than the tallest boy?

    (A) 25%
    (B) 50%
    (C) 62.5%
    (D) 66.7%
    (E) 75%

12. What is the range of the set $\left\{\frac{2}{3}, \frac{8}{11}, \frac{5}{8}, \frac{4}{7}, \frac{9}{13}\right\}$?

    Give your answer as a fraction. $\frac{\boxed{}}{\boxed{}}$

13. The value of 30 oobers equals the value of 12 darbles, and the value of 5 muxes equals the value of 20 oobers. What is the ratio of the value of 2 muxes to that of 1 darble?

    Give your answer as a fraction. $\frac{\boxed{}}{\boxed{}}$

14. In a race, at least 3 and at most 5 runners will vie for gold, silver, and bronze medals. Which of the following could represent the total number of unique ways to distribute the three medals among the participants?

    Indicate all such numbers.

    A 3
    B 6
    C 12
    D 24
    E 30
    F 60

10

15. Carla has $\frac{1}{4}$ more sweaters than cardigans, and $\frac{2}{5}$ fewer cardigans than turtlenecks. If she has at least one of each item, what is the minimum total number of *turtlenecks plus sweaters* that Carla could have?

    ☐

16. The 500 students in a class took an examination. Scores were given on an integer scale of 0–100. Jamal's score was 2 standard deviations above the mean score on the examination, and Charlie's score was at exactly the 5th percentile. The distribution of exam scores was approximately normal. Which of the following statements must be true?

    Indicate all such statements.

    A Jamal scored closer to the mean than Charlie.
    B More than 400 students achieved scores less than or equal to Jamal's score and greater than or equal to Charlie's score.
    C Fewer than 450 students achieved scores less than or equal to Jamal's score and greater than or equal to Charlie's score.
    D At least one other person received the same score as Charlie.

17. The probability of Tom rolling a strike while bowling is 40% on any given frame. If Tom rolls 4 frames in a row, which of the following statements are true?

    Indicate all such statements.

    A The probability of Tom rolling a strike on all 4 frames is greater than 3%.
    B The probability of Tom rolling no strikes in 4 frames is less than 10%.
    C Tom is equally likely to roll exactly 1 strike as to roll exactly 2 strikes in those 4 frames.
    D Tom will roll 2 or more strikes less than half the time.

18. It takes *h* minutes to fill a hot tub with a hot water hose and *c* minutes to fill it with a cold water hose, where *c* is smaller than *h*.

Quantity A	**Quantity B**
$\dfrac{h^2}{c+h}$	The number of minutes required to fill the hot tub using the hot water hose and the cold water hose simultaneously

19. 1,500 individuals attended a marathon held in Town A. Of those, only *y* participated in the marathon. If *x* of the 1,500 individuals were from Town A, and *z* of the individiuals participated in the marathon but were not from Town A, which of the following represents the number of individuals who did not participate in the marathon and were not from Town A?

   (A) $1,500 - x + 2y$
   (B) $1,500 - x + 2z$
   (C) $1,500 - x - y + z$
   (D) $1,500 - x + y - z$
   (E) $1,500 - x - z$

20. How many 3-digit integers can be chosen such that none of the digits appear more than twice, and none of the digits equal 0?

   (A) 729
   (B) 720
   (C) 648
   (D) 640
   (E) 576

Hard Practice Question Solutions

1.   **(A):** In this problem, you have two unknowns: the number of five-inch pieces and the number of seven-inch pieces. However, you only have one equation to relate them, namely, that the total length of the various pieces must equal 135 inches. In general such a problem should be unsolvable, but there is a hidden constraint: that the number of pieces must be integers, with no remaining steel left over. Thus, there is a solution (in fact, multiple solutions), and since the question asks for the minimum number of five-inch steel pieces, you can find that single solution.

Note that a "trade" is possible between 7 five-inch pieces and 5 seven-inch pieces; they each equal 35 inches. You can start the solution process by noting that it is possible to make up 135 inches by using 27 five-inch pieces and no seven-inch pieces. Afterwards, you can keep trading 7 five-inch pieces for 5 seven-inch pieces in order to generate further solutions. The table below shows the possibilities:

Number of Five-Inch Pieces	Number of Seven-Inch Pieces
27	0
20	5
13	10
6	15

Because a further trade is impossible (you cannot have a negative number of five-inch pieces), the minimum possible number of five-inch pieces is 6. Therefore, **Quantity A is greater**.

2.   **(B):** The probability that the first two socks will be brown is $\dfrac{6}{10} \times \dfrac{5}{9}$, which equals $\dfrac{30}{90}$, whereas the probability that the first two socks will be black is $\dfrac{4}{10} \times \dfrac{3}{9}$, which equals $\dfrac{12}{90}$. (These calculations reflect the Domino Effect of probability problems without replacement, in which the probability of an event is affected by a previous event—namely, the previous sock being removed from the drawer.)

The total probability of matching socks is given by $\dfrac{6}{10} \times \dfrac{5}{9} + \dfrac{4}{10} \times \dfrac{3}{9} = \dfrac{42}{90} = \dfrac{7}{15}$.

3.   **(A):** This problem is well-suited to the "$1 - x$" shortcut. You can calculate the probability of each of the four rolls resulting in a *different* number each time as follows: The first roll is assigned a probability of 1, since the first number that comes up will not be the same as that of any previous roll (because there has been no previous roll). In the next roll, the first number that came up must be excluded, so that there are 5 allowable outcomes. Likewise, the third roll will have 4 allowable outcomes, and the fourth roll will have 3 allowable outcomes. The overall probability of all four numbers being distinct is therefore equal to $1 \times \dfrac{5}{6} \times \dfrac{4}{6} \times \dfrac{3}{6} = 1 \times \dfrac{5}{6} \times \dfrac{\cancel{4}}{3} \times \dfrac{1}{\cancel{2}} = \dfrac{5}{18}$. Thus, the probability of at least two rolls resulting in the same number is $1 - \dfrac{5}{18} = \dfrac{13}{18}$. You can determine that this number is greater than 70% (or 0.7) by using the GRE on-screen Calculator: $\dfrac{13}{18} = 0.7222\overline{2}$.

4. **45:** In order to solve this multi-part Ratio problem, you must first establish a common term. As given, the number of managers appears as 3 in one ratio and as 5 in the other. The least common multiple of 3 and 5 is 15. Thus, by multiplying the first ratio by 5 and the second ratio by 3, you can make the number of managers the same, enabling you to combine the two ratios into one:

$$W : M = 20 : 3 = 100 : 15 \text{ and } M : D = 5 : 1 = 15 : 3, \text{ so that } W : M : D = 100 : 15 : 3$$

So, for every 3 directors, there will be 15 managers and 100 workers. Thus, a "unit" of employees is $3 + 15 + 100 = 118$. From this, you see that the total number of employees will need to be some integer multiple of 118. The only such number between 300 and 400 is 3×118, which is 354. Thus, the number of managers will be given by the same multiplier: $3 \times 15 = 45$.

5. **7:** The median value of the six integers other than x is the average of the two middle terms: $\dfrac{5+7}{2} = 6$. If x is 5 or less, the median of the set of seven numbers will be 5. If x is 7 or greater, the median of the seven numbers will be 7. Finally, if x is 6, then the median of the seven numbers will be 6.

You can test these cases:

Value of x	Current Median of the Whole Set	Median If x Decreases by 1	Median If x Increases by 1
5	5	5	6
6	6	5	7
7	7	6	7

From these observations, you can see that the only way for the median to stay *unchanged* when x increases, but to *decrease by* 1 when x decreases, is for x to equal 7. (Note that if x is 4 or less, or 8 or more, the median will not change at all when x increases or decreases by 1.)

6. **3.5:** Sally's rate of work is half of Jaya's rate of 40 pancakes per minute, and is thus 20 pancakes per minute. Using the Work equation $R \times t = W$, you can solve for the time that Sally flips the first 30 pancakes: $t_1 = \dfrac{W}{R} = \dfrac{30}{20} = 1\dfrac{1}{2}$ minutes. After Sally is joined by Jaya, the two work at the *combined* rate of 60 pancakes per minute, flipping the remaining 120 pancakes in $t_2 = \dfrac{W}{R} = \dfrac{120}{60} = 2$ minutes.

Their total time to flip 150 pancakes is therefore equal to the sum of format $1\dfrac{1}{2} + 2 = 3\dfrac{1}{2} = 3.5$ minutes.

10

MANHATTAN
PREP

7. **(B):** Probably the most effective way to solve this problem is to use an *RTD* chart. In setting up the chart, use units of miles and hours; therefore, the 40 minutes will need to be written as $\frac{40}{60} = \frac{2}{3}$ hours to be consistent. Define t as the time, in hours, that Jake spends riding his bike. In that case, he must spend $\frac{2}{3} - t$ hours walking.

The *RTD* chart will look like this:

Travel	R (miles/hour)	T (hours)	D (miles)
Bike	10	t	$10t$
Walk	3	$\frac{2}{3} - t$	$3\left(\frac{2}{3} - t\right) = 2 - 3t$
Total	*N/A*	$\frac{2}{3}$	$(10t) + (2 - 3t) = 7t + 2$

In order to solve for t, you need to use the fact that Jake travels $\frac{2}{3}$ of the distance on his bike and $\frac{1}{3}$ of the distance on foot. Thus, the distance he travels on his bike is two times the distance he travels on foot: $10t = 2(2 - 3t) = 4 - 6t$, such that $16t = 4$ and $t = \frac{1}{4}$ hour. The total distance that Jake travels is then $7t + 2 = 7\left(\frac{1}{4}\right) + 2 = \frac{15}{4}$ miles.

(Note that this chart could also be set up with *t as the column solved for, and d as the variable.*)

8. **60:** There are a two primary ways to approach this problem (each with its own intuitive appeal). Before solving the problem, note that if order did not matter at all, Jasper could choose a total of 5 committees. The formula for (5 Choose 4) is $\frac{5!}{4! \times 1!} = 5$. If, on the other hand, order always mattered, Jasper could choose a total of 120 committees: $\frac{5!}{1!} = 120$.

You cannot use either formula here since order matters with respect to some of the selections, but not for others. To see this, think of Jasper drawing names out of a hat, assigning President to the first name chosen, Vice President to second name chosen, and Treasurer to the third and fourth names chosen. Notice that the order of the first two selections matters (as it determines which person is the President and which person is the Vice President), but order does *not* matter for the next two selections (picking a certain person as the first Treasurer is the same as choosing him or her as the second Treasurer). Based on this, you know that the number of committees should be greater than 5 but less than 120.

Solution method 1: There are 5 ways to choose a President from among the 5 candidates. Once a President has been chosen, there are 4 ways to choose a Vice President (since there are only 4 candidates remaining after the President has been selected). There are then 3 candidates remaining from which to choose 2 Treasurers, which is equivalent to choosing which 1 of the 3 will not be Treasurer. There are 3 ways to omit 1 person, implying that there are 3 ways to choose 2 Treasurers. Therefore, the answer is $5 \times 4 \times 3$, which is 60.

Solution method 2:

Create an Anagram Grid:

Candidate	A	B	C	D	E
Role	P	V	T	T	N

Where P stands for President, V for Vice President, T for the two Treasurers, and N for Not Selected.

There are $\dfrac{5!}{1! \times 1! \times 2! \times 1!} = \dfrac{5 \times 4 \times 3 \times 2 \times 1}{2} = 5 \times 4 \times 3 = 60$ different possible committees.

9. **(E):** First, notice that 4 attendees will not donate $1,200, as each person would donate only $220 ($300 minus $20 for each attendee) for a total of $880. If 5 guests attend, each will donate $200, for a total of $1,000. If 6 guests attend, each will donate $180, for a total of $1,080. If 7 guests attend, each will donate $160, for a total of $1,120. If 8 guests attend, each will donate $140, for a total of $1,120. In table form:

Number of Guests Attending Event	Donation per Attendee	Total Contribution
4	$220	$880
5	200	1,000
6	180	1,080
7	160	**1,120**
8	140	**1,120**
9	120	1,080

As can be seen, beyond 8 attendees, the per-attendee donation is falling faster than the number of attendees is rising, so the total contribution is falling. Thus, the maximum that can be raised at this fundraiser is $1,120, which is not enough money to build the park. The correct answer is (E).

10. **(B):** You want to minimize trippim, so you should maximize the other coins, beginning with the megam because you want to keep the number of coins low. Divide $3.21 by 19 cents and find the remainder: $\dfrac{\$3.21}{\$0.19} = 16$, with a remainder of 17 (i.e., $16\dfrac{17}{19}$). This means that, if you select 16 megam, you must still account for 17 cents. Since 17 is odd, you cannot account for this remainder entirely with 2-cent duom, so you must include one trippim. One trippim would account for 11 of the 17 cents, and three duom would account for the other 6 cents. This allows 16 megam, 1 trippim, and

3 duom, for a total of 20 coins. Since 17 is an odd number, you must have one trippim and therefore three duom, making 20 coins exactly.

It can be shown, incidentally, that no other combination of coins can exist such that the man has 20 coins or fewer.

11. **(C):** Given the information about the fraction of boys who are shorter than the shortest girl and the fraction of girls who are taller than the tallest boy, the number of boys in the class must be a multiple of 5 while the number of girls must be a multiple of 3 (since the number of boys and girls must take on integer values).

The only combination of a multiple of 5 and multiple of 3 that sum to 16 is $2 \times 5 = 10$ boys and $2 \times 3 = 6$ girls. Of the 10 boys, 2 are shorter than the shortest girl. Of the 6 girls, 2 are taller than the tallest boy. Therefore, the order of heights must be as follows:

$$B, B, G, \_\ \_\ \_\ \_\ \_\ \_\ \_\ \_\ \_\ \_, B, G, G$$

This implies that there must be exactly 10 students that are taller than the shortest girl and shorter than the tallest boy. This equals $\dfrac{10}{16} = \dfrac{5}{8} = 62.5\%$.

12. $\dfrac{12}{77}$ **(or any fractional equivalent):** In order to find the range of the set, you must first determine the largest and smallest members of the set. You can compare the fractions in pairs to determine which is the larger in each pair. Note that, to quickly compare two fractions, you can cross-multiply the numerators and denominators and write the results next to the numerators. Whichever product is greater will indicate which fraction is greater.

For example, comparing $\dfrac{2}{3}$ to $\dfrac{8}{11}$, cross-multiply. This comparison is the same as comparing to 2×11 to 8×3: $22 < 24$, so $\dfrac{2}{3} < \dfrac{8}{11}$.

Proceeding likewise, you can determine that $\dfrac{8}{11}$ is, in fact, the largest of all the fractions, whereas $\dfrac{4}{7}$ is the smallest. The range of the set is the difference between the largest and the smallest members:

$$\frac{8}{11} - \frac{4}{7} = \frac{8 \times 7 - 4 \times 11}{77} = \frac{56 - 44}{77} = \frac{12}{77}$$

13. $\dfrac{16}{5}$ **(or any fractional equivalent):** The given facts can be written as $30O = 12D$ and $5M = 20O$.

You need to relate muxes to darbles, so you need to eliminate oobers from the system of equations. This will be simpler if the same multiple of oobers appears in each equation. The least common multiple of 30 and 20 is 60, so multiply the first equation by 2 and the second equation by 3:

$$60O = 24D \text{ and } 15M = 60O$$

Equating, you obtain $24D = 15M$.

You can turn this equation into the ratio of muxes to darbles by dividing by 15 and by D:

$\dfrac{M}{D} = \dfrac{24}{15} = \dfrac{8}{5}$. The ratio of two muxes to one darble is twice that, or $\dfrac{16}{5}$. (Note that it is not necessary to fully reduce fractions in order to get credit for a right answer; fractions such as $\dfrac{32}{10}$ or $\dfrac{48}{15}$ are also considered correct.)

14. **(B)**, **(D)**, and **(F)**: Use the Anagram Grid to determine the number of possible ways to award the three medals. Let G, S, and B represent the medalists and N represent non-medalists (if any). Also, you can use numbers to designate the participants. If there are three participants, the Anagram Grid looks like this:

1	2	3
G	S	B

The total number of ways to award the medals in this case is 3!: $3 \times 2 \times 1 = 6$. If there are four participants, the grid looks like:

1	2	3	4
G	S	B	N

In this case the total number of possibilities equals 4!: $4 \times 3 \times 2 \times 1 = 24$. Lastly, when there are five participants, the grid looks like:

1	2	3	4	5
G	S	B	N	N

Here there is a repeated letter N; thus, the number of possible anagrams is found as $\dfrac{5!}{2!} : \dfrac{5 \times 4 \times 3 \times 2 \times 1}{2 \times 1} = \dfrac{120}{2} = 60$.

15. **35:** You can express the given relationships as $S = C + \dfrac{1}{4}C = \dfrac{5}{4}C$ and $C = T - \dfrac{2}{5}T = \dfrac{3}{5}T$. You can reverse the latter to yield $T = \dfrac{5}{3}C$. You can now use the hidden constraint in the problem: the number of each item of clothing has to be an integer. Thus, the number C of cardigans has to be divisible both by 4 (to yield an integer number of sweaters) and by 3 (to yield an integer number of turtlenecks). The smallest number is 12, which is the least common multiple of 4 and 3. With $C = 12$, you can obtain $S = 15$ and $T = 20$, so at minimum, $S + T = 35$.

16. **(B) and (D):** Choice (A) is incorrect because 2 standard deviations above the mean is at approximately the 98th percentile, or 48 percentile points away from the mean. By contrast, Charlie's score was 45 percentile points away from the mean since the distribution is approximately normal, and thus it is also approximately symmetric.

10

Choice (B) is correct. If Jamal's score places him at approximately the 98th percentile and Charlie's score was at the 5th percentile, then about 93% of the class scored between Jamal and Charlie since 93% of 500 is equal to 465.

(For the same reason, choice (C) is incorrect.)

Choice (D) is the toughest to evaluate. By definition, each percentile encompasses 5 scores (when the scores are ranked from lowest to highest). The percentile is defined as the score that separates the highest score in the preceding percentile from the lowest score in the next percentile. Thus, for example, in a class of 500, the 1st percentile score would be defined as the average of the 5th lowest and 6th lowest scores. Similarly, Charlie's score equals the average of the 25th and 26th lowest scores on the test. Those two values have to be equal, because Charlie's score had to be an integer and had to be equal in value to either the 25th or 26th highest score. Thus, at least one other student received exactly the same score as Charlie.

To use a numerical example, say the 25th lowest score was a 30 and the 26th lowest score was a 31. Then the 5th percentile would be defined as 30.5—an impossible score to obtain, because all scores were given on an integer scale between 0 and 100. If the 25th lowest score was a 30 and the 26th lowest score was a 32, then Charlie would have had to score a 31, which would put him in between the 25th and 26th lowest scores. This, too, is impossible, because then Charlie would not have scored the 25th or 26th lowest score—and he has to have a score equal to *one* of them! Thus, to put it succinctly, Charlie's score *had* to match that of the 25th lowest and the 26th lowest scores, making them equal, and meaning that *at least* one other student received the same score Charlie received.

17. **(C):** The key to answering this question is to be able to calculate the probability of rolling exactly 0, 1, 2, 3, and 4 strikes in the 4 frames he rolls.

The easiest probability to calculate is the probability of rolling a strike 4 times in a row. Denote that as P(*SSSS*), (i.e., the probability of 4 strikes (*S*) in a row). By the "AND" principle, you should multiply the probability of rolling a strike 4 times: $(40\%)(40\%)(40\%)(40\%) = 0.4^4 = 0.0256$, or 2.56%.

Thus, choice (A) is incorrect—Tom's probability of rolling 4 strikes in a row is less than 3%.

Next easiest is to calculate the probability of 4 non-strikes in a row. Denote that as P(*NNNN*), (i.e., the probability of 4 non-strikes (*N*) in a row). By the "1 – *x*" principle, the probability of a non-strike is $1 - 40\% = 60\%$. By the "AND" principle, you should multiply the probability of rolling a non-strike 4 times: $(60\%)(60\%)(60\%)(60\%) = 0.6^4 = 0.1296$, or 12.96%. Thus, choice (B) is incorrect—Tom's probability of rolling no strikes at all is greater than 10%.

Calculating 1, 2, or 3 strikes is more difficult. Evaluate one scenario: Tom rolls a strike in the first frame, and then non-strikes in the subsequent frames. The probability of this is P(*SNNN*) = (40%) (60%)(60%)(60%) = $0.4^1 \times 0.6^3 = 0.0864$. However, Tom can get exactly 1 strike in 4 different ways: 1) get a strike on frame 1, 2) get a strike on frame 2, 3) get a strike on frame 3, or 4) get a strike on frame 4. Since these probabilities are all equal, you can simply take $4 \times 0.0864 = 0.3456 = 34.56\%$.

 This is the probability of getting exactly 1 strike on any of the frames.

Incidentally, you can now disprove choice (D). Since Tom will get no strikes 12.96% of the time and 1 strike 34.56% of the time, he will get 2 or more strikes 100% − 12.96% − 34.56% = 52.48% of the time.

To calculate 2 strikes, follow similar logic. The probability of (*SSNN*), strikes on the first two frames only, is $(40\%)(40\%)(60\%)(60\%) = 0.4^2 \times 0.6^2 = 0.0576$. However, *SSNN* is an anagram, and there are thus $\dfrac{4!}{2! \times 2!} = \dfrac{4 \times 3 \times 2 \times 1}{(2 \times 1)(2 \times 1)} = \dfrac{12}{2} = 6$ different ways to get exactly two strikes. The odds of exactly 2 strikes are thus $6 \times 0.0576 = 0.3456 = 34.56\%$. This is *exactly* equal to the odds of rolling 1 strike, so choice (C) is correct.

Incidentally, the odds of rolling exactly 3 strikes, following the same logic, is $4 \times$ P(*SSSN*) =

$4 \times (40\%)(40\%)(40\%)(60\%) = 4 \times 0.4^3 \times 0.6^1 = 15.36\%$.

18. **(A):** If it takes the hot water hose h minutes to fill the hot tub, then it fills $\dfrac{1}{h}$ of the hot tub per minute. Similarly, if it takes the cold water hose c minutes to fill the hot tub, then it fills $\dfrac{1}{c}$ of the hot tub per minute. Working combined, they fill $\dfrac{1}{h} + \dfrac{1}{c} = \dfrac{c + h}{hc}$ of the hot tub per minute. In other words, it will take $\dfrac{hc}{c + h}$ minutes to fill the hot tub.

Therefore, the comparison becomes:

Quantity A	**Quantity B**
$\dfrac{h^2}{c + h}$	$\dfrac{hc}{c + h}$

Since $c < h$ and both c and h must be positive, **Quantity A is greater**.

19. **(E):** The parts of the Venn diagram corresponding to this description are as follows:

Total Attending Town A Marathon: 1,500 people

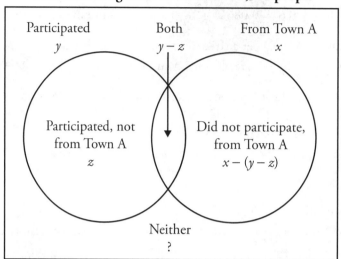

Thus, you need to subtract the values inside the circles from 1,500 to arrive at the number of individuals who neither are from Town A nor participated in the marathon. This is equal to $x + y$, minus the overlap region, which is $(y - z)$. The quantity inside the circles is thus $[y + x - (y - z)]$. The correct answer is therefore: $1,500 - [y + x - (y - z)] = 1500 - y - x + y - z = 1,500 - x - z$. Choice (E) is correct.

20. **(B):** The easiest way to calculate this problem is to think in terms of the Slot Method. Each of the 3 digits can be filled by one of 9 numbers; each of 3 slots has thus 9 different options. By the Fundamental Counting Principle, you multiply the number of options for each choice to solve for the total number of possible choices: $9 \times 9 \times 9 = 729$.

However, this will erroneously include the scenarios where all 3 digits are the same. You need to subtract those possibilities out. To determine how many such options there are, you need to again consider the Slot Method. There are 9 possible values (each of the digits 1–9) that will satisfy the constraint that all 3 digits are the same. However, once that slot has been filled, each of the remaining slots now only has one choice: the same digit that was selected for the first slot. Thus, there are $9 \times 1 \times 1 = 9$ possible 3-digit integers where all 3 digits are the same.

Subtracting these 9 integers out, you get a result of $729 - 9 = 720$ integers that fit the question. Choice (B) is the correct answer.

STUDY ANYWHERE!

WITH MANHATTAN PREP'S GRE FLASH CARDS

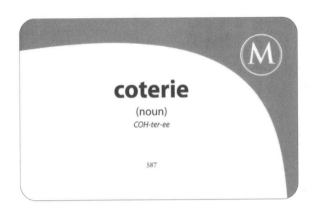

coterie

(noun)

COH-ter-ee

587

Definition: Close or exclusive group, clique

Usage: The pop star never traveled anywhere without a **coterie** of assistants and managers.

Related Words: *Cabal* (conspiracy, group of people who plot), *Entourage* (group of attendants)

More Info: In French, a *coterie* was a group of tenant farmers.

With our flashcards you can study both math and verbal concepts on the go!

Both our 500 Essential Words and a 500 Advanced Words cards go above and beyond providing abstract, out-of-context definitions. Complete with definitions, example sentences, pronunciations, and related words, this two-volume set comprises the most comprehensive vocabulary study tool on the market.

Our GRE Math Flash Cards provide practical exposure to the basic math concepts tested on the GRE.

Designed to be user-friendly for all students, these cards include easy-to-follow explanations of math concepts that promise to enhance comprehension and build fundamental skills.

For the revised GRE

M

MANHATTAN PREP

GRE® FLASH CARDS

500 Math Flash Cards

✓ Designed specifically for the math question types found on the revised GRE

✓ Cards cover all tested content and include clear, efficient explanations

✓ Want Verbal? Check out our flash card sets *500 Essential Words* & *500 Advanced Words*

GRE is a registered trademark of the Educational Testing Service (ETS), which neither sponsors nor endorses this test product.

NEED MORE THAN BOOKS ALONE?

TRY OUR GUIDED SELF-STUDY PROGRAM!

With over 27 hours of recorded video lessons, Guided Self-Study is a perfect fit for self-motivated individuals who want full access to all of Manhattan Prep's materials.

Armed with our syllabus and online resources suite, you can get more out of your books. This program is a great fit for students operating under a tight deadline or rigid schedule who may not have the time to take a live prep course.

Check it out at manhattanprep.com/gre/gre-self-study.cfm